MARVEL

CAPTAIN AMERICA

THE FIRST AVENGER

THE SCREENPLAY

BY
CHRISTOPHER MARKUS
&STEPHEN MCFEELY

MARVEL

CAPTAIN AMERICA

THE FIRST AVENGER

THE SCREENPLAY

MARVEL'S CAPTAIN AMERICA: THE FIRST AVENGER — THE SCREENPLAY. Published by MARVEL WORLDWIDE, INC., a subsidiary of MARVEL ENTERTAINMENT, LLC. OFFICE OF PUBLICATION: 135 West 50th Street, New York, NY 10020. Copyright © 2014 Marvel Characters, Inc. All rights reserved.

ISBN# 978-0-7851-5441-9

Printed in the U.S.A.

ALAN FINE, EVP - Office of the President, Marvel Worldwide, Inc. and EVP & CMO Marvel Characters B.V.; DAN BUCKLEY, Publisher & President - Print, Animation & Digital Divisions; JOE QUESADA, Chief Creative Officer; TOM BREVOORT, SVP of Publishing; DAVID BOGART, SVP of Operations & Procurement, Publishing; C.B. CEBULSKI, SVP of Creator & Content Development; DAVID GABRIEL, SVP of Print & Digital Publishing Sales; JIM O'KEEFE, VP of Operations & Logistics; DAN CARR, Executive Director of Publishing Technology; SUSAN CRESPI, Editorial Operations Manager; ALEX MORALES, Publishing Operations Manager; STAN LEE, Chairman Emeritus. For information regarding advertising in Marvel Comics or on Marvel.com, please contact Niza Disla, Director of Marvel Partnerships, at ndisla@marvel.com. For Marvel subscription inquiries, please call 800-217-9158. **Manufactured between 1/3/2014 and 2/10/2014 by SHERIDAN BOOKS, INC., CHELSEA, MI, USA.**

First printing 2014
10 9 8 7 6 5 4 3 2 1

CAPTAIN AMERICA CREATED BY JOE SIMON AND JACK KIRBY

COVER DESIGN BY JEFF POWELL
INTERIOR DESIGN BY NELSON RIBEIRO

FOR MARVEL PUBLISHING
JEFF YOUNGQUIST, Editor
SARAH BRUNSTAD, Assistant Editor
ALEX STARBUCK, Associate Managing Editor
DAVID GABRIEL, SVP Print, Sales & Marketing
AXEL ALONSO, Editor in Chief
JOE QUESADA, Chief Creative Officer
DAN BUCKLEY, Publisher
ALAN FINE, Executive Producer

FOR MARVEL STUDIOS
KEVIN FEIGE, President
LOUIS D'ESPOSITO, Co-President
VICTORIA ALONSO, Executive Vice President, Visual Effects
STEPHEN BROUSSARD, Senior Vice President, Production & Development
WILL CORONA PILGRIM, Creative Manager, Research & Development

SPECIAL THANKS TO ERICA DENTON & GREGORY BALDWIN

CONTENTS

FROSTBITE

by

Christopher Markus
&
Stephen McFeely

FINAL SHOOTING DRAFT

FADE IN:

1 EXT. FROZEN WASTELAND - DAY

Snow whips. Headlights approach. A HIGH-TECH
HMUV grinds through an ARCTIC SNOWSTORM.
The HMUV stops. TWO SHIELD MEN get out.
The whipping snow is deafening. They can barely
see.
THE SEARCH TEAM LEADER, a CIVILIAN, meets them,
offering his hand.

> SEARCH TEAM LEADER
> (shouting over the wind)
> You the guys from Washington?

> SHIELD LT.
> That's some flight.
> ALT. Get many other visitors out here?

> SHIELD TECH
> How long have you been on site?

> SEARCH TEAM LEADER
> Since this morning. A Russian oil team
> called it in about 18 hours ago.

> SHIELD LT.
> How come nobody spotted it before?

> SEARCH TEAM LEADER
> (gesturing around them)
> Ice melts. Storms blow in.
> Landscape changes all the time.

The Search Leader gets a worried look.

> SEARCH TEAM LEADER (CONT'D)
> You mind if I ask what this thing is,
> exactly?

SHIELD LT.
Would you believe us if we said it was a
weather balloon?

SEARCH TEAM LEADER
No.

The SHIELD men stare. The team leader shrugs and
walks on.

SEARCH TEAM LEADER (CONT'D)
Listen, for the record, I'm not sure we
have the equipment for a job like this—

SHIELD LT.
Is the sonar up and running yet?

SEARCH TEAM LEADER
Sure. We're getting deep ice preliminaries
now. Very deep.

SHIELD TECH
So? How long before we can start craning
it out?

He stops the Shield Tech, a bit incredulous.

SEARCH TEAM LEADER
I don't think you quite understand...

The Search Team Leader points at something off
screen.

SEARCH TEAM LEADER (CONT'D)
You guys are going to need one hell of a
crane.

THE TWO SHIELD MEN look off screen, awestruck.

REVEAL: A MASSIVE WINGTIP JUTS FROM THE ICE,
TOWERING ABOVE THEM LIKE A SKYSCRAPER.

A SKULL AND TENTACLE LOGO is just visible
through the ice.
German words are stenciled ominously below.

2 OMITTED

3 OMITTED

4 INT. FROZEN PLANE - NIGHT

PITCH BLACK. The laser burns through, cutting a
hole. The metal circle drops, letting in a shaft
of light.

THE TWO SHIELD OPERATIVES FROM THE HMUV RAPPEL
DOWN ON ROPES.

They creep through THE FROZEN, DEVASTATED PLANE.

Shattered control screens reflect their
flashlights.

THE LIEUTENANT eyes a panel, "GEFAHR.
EXPLOSIVSTOFFE."

> SHIELD LT. (INTO RADIO)
> This has got to be World War II.
> But the Luftwaffe didn't have anything
> nearly this advanced.
> (beat)
> Or this big.

> SHIELD TECH
> Lieutenant?

> SHIELD LT. (INTO RADIO)
> Hold that, Base.

THE TECH chips at AN ICE FLOE, then stops.

                    SHIELD TECH
          What is it?

The lieutenant stares, awed.

                    SHIELD LT. (INTO RADIO)
          Base, get me a line to the colonel.
          I don't care what time it is.
          (beat)
          This one's worth waking up for.

He knocks away the last of the ice,
revealing...A RED, WHITE AND BLUE SHIELD.

5 EXT. FROZEN WASTELAND - NIGHT

A SNOWCAT HAULS OUT A HUGE BLOCK OF ICE. THE
SHIELD IS BARELY VISIBLE INSIDE.

6 EXT. CASTLE ROCK TOWER - NIGHT

TWO PARTISANS race across the cobblestones. AN
OMINOUS CLANKING FILLS THE AIR.

                    ERIK
          (subtitled Norwegian)
          Go and tell the Keeper! Hurry!

TITLE: "NORWAY, MAY 1942."

JAN RUNS. ERIK sets a MOLOTOV down and checks
his rifle.
THE MOLOTOV TOPPLES ON THE COBBLESTONES. THE
OMINOUS CLANKING RISES UNTIL...
A HUGE TANK, THE LANDKREUZER, CRASHES THROUGH A
BUILDING.

Erik pales at the HYDRA LOGO. He runs, but
MACHINE GUNS CUT HIM DOWN.

6A EXT. CASTLE ROCK TOWER - NIGHT

Jan races toward the front door of a lonely
STONE TOWER.

7 INT. CASTLE ROCK TOWER - NIGHT

Jan slams down a huge timber crossbeam, locking
the door.

                    JAN
        They're coming!

AN OLD TOWER KEEPER rushes downstairs.

                    TOWER KEEPER
        They'll never find it.

The two men turn as...THE OMINOUS CLANKING RISES
OUTSIDE. THE LANDKREUZER PUNCHES THROUGH THE
WALL. BRICKS AND TIMBER RAIN DOWN, KNOCKING THE
KEEPER BACK. WHEN THE DUST SUBSIDES, THE KEEPER
STRUGGLES TO HIS FEET, ONLY TO FIND JAN DEAD
AMIDST THE RUBBLE.

HYDRA TROOPS POUR IN, SURROUNDING HIM.

8 OMITTED

9 OMITTED

10 EXT. CASTLE ROCK TOWER - NIGHT

A MODIFIED CAR pulls up, ITS HOOD ORNAMENT A
HYDRA SKULL.
GLEAMING JACKBOOTS STEP OUT ONTO THE
COBBLESTONES.

11 INT. CASTLE ROCK TOWER - NIGHT

THE HYDRA SOLDIERS THROW THE KEEPER DOWN IN
FRONT OF A STONE SARCOPHAGUS IN AN ORNATE CRYPT.

The soldiers try but FAIL TO PUSH THE MASSIVE
COFFIN LID.

                    HYDRA LIEUTENANT
          Quickly, before he-

Then, FOOTSTEPS. The soldiers snap to attention
as...
A HYDRA OFFICER, JOHANN SCHMIDT, STEPS THROUGH
THE RUBBLE.
HIS EYES ARE SUNKEN, HIS SKIN PALE AND WAXY.

                    JOHANN SCHMIDT
          It has taken me a long time to find this
          place. You should be commended.

He stands before the tower keeper.

                    JOHANN SCHMIDT (CONT'D)
          Give me what I want, and you will find the
          Reich most appreciative.

                    TOWER KEEPER
          I give you nothing.

A HYDRA GUARD moves to clock the old man, but
Schmidt waves him off. He leans over the tower
keeper.

                    JOHANN SCHMIDT
          You are a man of great vision. In that, we
          are much alike.

                    TOWER KEEPER
          I am nothing like you.

                    JOHANN SCHMIDT
          Oh, no, no. I don't suggest that.

Schmidt sees his men struggling with the coffin
lid.

>   JOHANN SCHMIDT (CONT'D)
>   But what others see as superstition,
>   you and I know to be science. The oldest
>   science.

>   TOWER KEEPER
>   What you seek is just a legend.

>   JOHANN SCHMIDT
>   Then why do you try so hard to hide it?

Schmidt strides to the coffin. He heaves the
heavy lid aside.
It smashes to the floor.
Inside, A DESICCATED CORPSE holds...A CRYSTAL
CUBE.

>   JOHANN SCHMIDT (CONT'D)
>   The Tesseract was the Jewel of Odin's
>   treasure room.

He turns it over in his hand, curious...THEN
DROPS IT TO THE FLOOR. IT SHATTERS.

>   JOHANN SCHMIDT (CONT'D)
>   It is not a thing one buries.

HE LIFTS THE OLD MAN BY THE SHOULDER, HISSING IN
HIS EAR.

>   JOHANN SCHMIDT (CONT'D)
>   But it is close, yes?

>   TOWER KEEPER
>   I cannot help you.

>   JOHANN SCHMIDT
>   No. But you can help them.

He turns the old man to see THE TANK POINTING AT
THE TOWN.

> JOHANN SCHMIDT (CONT'D)
> You have friends out there. Grandchildren,
> perhaps. I've no need for them to die.

Terrified, the tower keeper lets his eyes flick to
A WALL.
Schmidt lets the old man down. HE SEARCHES THE
WALL, FINALLY LANDING ON THE CARVING OF A TREE.

> JOHANN SCHMIDT (CONT'D)
> Yggdrasil, tree of the world.
> Guardian of wisdom...

He scans the ROOTS, finally alighting on...A
SERPENT.

> JOHANN SCHMIDT (CONT'D)
> And fate.

He pushes the snake's eye, releasing A WOODEN
BOX CARVED LIKE A SNAKE. The old man sags,
defeated.

Schmidt opens the box. BLUE LIGHT illuminates
his face. He gazes, enraptured. The old man
stares, awed.

> JOHANN SCHMIDT (CONT'D)
> And the Fuhrer digs for the trinkets in
> the desert...

He looks over at the old man.

> JOHANN SCHMIDT (CONT'D)
> You've never seen it, have you?

> TOWER KEEPER
> It's not for the eyes of ordinary men.

> JOHANN SCHMIDT
> Exactly.

Schmidt shuts the box. The light disappears. He
glances over at the cannon, almost distractedly.

> JOHANN SCHMIDT (CONT'D)
> Commence firing.

A SOLDIER CALLS OUT OFF SCREEN AND THE CANNON
ERUPTS.
ENRAGED, THE OLD MAN LUNGES BUT IS HELD BACK BY
SOLDIERS.

> TOWER KEEPER
> Fool. None of us can control that power.
> You will burn.

> JOHANN SCHMIDT
> I already have.

SCHMIDT DRAWS HIS LUGER WITH DAZZLING SPEED.
BLAM. THE KEEPER DROPS.
The old man's blood has spattered Schmidt's
HYDRA LAPEL PIN.
His tentacled death's head is now A RED SKULL.

12 INT. ENLISTMENT OFFICE, BAYONNE, N.J. - DAY

A PAPER SCREAMS: "ELITE NAZI FORCES OVERRUN
NORWEGIAN TOWN."

> ARMY DOCTOR (O.S.)
> O'Connell, Michael...

The paper flaps down, revealing a young man. He
stands, wearing only boxer shorts.

TITLE: "NEW YORK CITY, JUNE 1943."

DOZENS OF HALF-DRESSED RECRUITS read newspapers,
waiting for their exam results.

ANOTHER PAPER: "U-BOATS TORPEDO SHIP OFF COAST OF VIRGINIA."

> ARMY DOCTOR (CONT'D)
> Kaminsky, Henry...

Kaminsky stands, tossing his paper aside. He glances at the next newsreader down.

CLOSE ON: THE PAPER, "NAZIS BURN CZECH VILLAGE TO THE GROUND."

> HENRY KAMINSKY
> Kinda makes you think twice about enlisting, huh?

STEVE ROGERS LOWERS HIS PAPER. He's frail and small.

> STEVE
> Nope.

> ARMY DOCTOR (O.S.)
> Rogers, Steven.

Steve folds the paper and gets to his feet.

TIME CUT:
Steve anxiously watches AN ARMY DOCTOR scan his file.
CLOSE ON: STEVE'S FILE. A dozen ailments have been checked.

> ARMY DOCTOR (CONT'D)
> What did your father die of?

> STEVE
> Mustard gas.

The doctor looks up.

> STEVE (CONT'D)
> 1918. He was in the 107th Infantry. I was hoping to get assigned to them if—

> ARMY DOCTOR
> And your mother?

> STEVE
> Few years back, she was a nurse in the TB ward. Got hit, couldn't shake it.

Finally, THE DOCTOR SHAKES HIS HEAD.

> STEVE (CONT'D)
> They weren't weak, Doc; they were fighters. If you just give me a—

> ARMY DOCTOR
> Sorry, son. You'd be ineligible on your asthma alone.

> STEVE
> You can't do anything?

> ARMY DOCTOR
> I'm doing it. I'm saving your life.

THE DOCTOR STAMPS STEVE'S FILE: 4F.

13 INT. MOVIE THEATER, NEW YORK CITY - DAY

SPINNING MATCH CUT: A SWASTIKA FLUTTERS ON A FLAG. A NEWSREEL FLICKERS. A COLUMN OF NAZIS STOMPS DOWN A ROAD.

> NEWSREEL ANNOUNCER
> As Hitler's troops continue to ravage Occupied Europe...

Steve sits in the audience, watching intently.

NEWSREEL ANNOUNCER (CONT'D)
On the home front, enlistment centers teem
with the able-bodied, eager to help our
allies

A LINE OF MEN SNAKES OUT A RECRUITING OFFICE.

LOUD JERK (O.S.)
They're just tryin' to get outa workin'
for a living.

A FEW ROWS AHEAD, A MAN SHOUTS BACK AT THE
SCREEN.

Steve looks across the aisle. A YOUNG WOMAN
watches the screen, tears welling. She clearly
has a man overseas.
Across the aisle, a middle-aged Jewish couple
looks somber.

NEWSREEL ANNOUNCER
Across the seas, our brave boys are already
showing the Axis that the price of freedom
is never too high!

Soldiers—some wounded—wave at the camera, their
smiles almost convincing.

LOUD JERK (O.S.)
Jeez, play the cartoon, already!

Steve sees the woman flinch. He whispers to the
man:

STEVE
Can you keep it down, please?

NEWSREEL ANNOUNCER
Together with the allied forces, they march
toward freedom and liberation for millions
of grateful citizens.

A KID PULLS HIS WAGON. A HAND-DRAWN SIGN SAYS
"SCRAP METAL."

> LOUD JERK (O.S.)
> Let 'em clean up their own mess, the
> jerks!

Steve leans over, fuming. He jabs the man in the
shoulder.

> STEVE
> YOU WANT TO SHUT UP?

The man slowly rises from his slumped position.
He rises...and rises, revealing...
A VERY LARGE JERK.

14 EXT. MOVIE THEATER, ALLEY - LATE AFTERNOON

WHAM! The jerk hammers Steve in the jaw,
knocking him into a line of garbage cans. Steve
groans...and GETS BACK UP. Steve's a natural
fighter, bobbing and scoring a kidney punch, but
the guy barely feels it. The jerk swings. STEVE
tries to BLOCK WITH A TRASH CAN LID. The jerk
yanks away the lid and pounds him again. Steve's
feet lift off the ground.
HE HITS THE CEMENT HARD. For a moment, Steve
lays still. The jerk hovers, panting.
THEN STEVE GETS TO HIS FEET AGAIN. The jerk
shakes his head.

> LOUD JERK
> You just don't know when to give up, do
> you?

> STEVE
> (wiping his bloody mouth)
> I can do this all day.

The jerk knocks Steve back into a pile of
garbage. He moves to hit him...BUT SOMEONE GRABS
HIS ARM.

                   BUCKY (O.S.)
       What's with all the fighting?

The jerk spins to see A SOLDIER, JAMES "BUCKY"
BARNES.

                   BUCKY (CONT'D)
       Don't you know there's a war on?

The jerk takes a swing. Bucky SLUGS him, spins
him around, and PLANTS an army boot in his ass.
The jerk runs away.
Bucky looks down at Steve, getting up from a
pile of garbage.

                   BUCKY (CONT'D)
       Sometimes I think you like getting punched.

                   STEVE
       I had him on the ropes.

As Steve gets up, a folded ENLISTMENT FORM falls
from his pocket. Bucky picks it up and reads.

                   BUCKY
       How many times is this?
       (reads)
       And you're from Paramus now? It's still
       illegal to lie on an enlistment form, and
       seriously, Jersey?

Steve frowns, TAKING IN BUCKY'S UNIFORM.

                   STEVE
       Looks like you got your orders.

                         BUCKY
          107th ships to England first thing tomorrow.
          (beat)
          This is my last night.

                         STEVE
          So, what's the first stop. Church?

Bucky grins.

                         BUCKY
          Yeah...maybe second stop.

They start walking out of the alley.

                         STEVE
          Where are we going?

He whips out a newspaper and hands it to Steve.

                         BUCKY
          The future.

Steve opens the paper. An ad reads, "WORLD
EXHIBITION OF TOMORROW." MONORAILS RACE AROUND
FUTURISTIC BUILDINGS.

DISSOLVE TO:

15 OMITTED

**16 EXT. WORLD EXPOSITION OF TOMORROW, MIDWAY -
NIGHT**

A MONORAIL SPEEDS OVER AN EPIC FAIR. Steve and
Bucky walk down the busy midway.

                         BUCKY
          I don't see what the problem is.
          You're about to be the last eligible man

in New York. You know there're three and a
half million women here?

STEVE
I'd settle for just one.

Bucky waves at somebody in the distance.

BUCKY
Good thing I've taken care of that.

Across the midway, TWO GIRLS WAVE BACK in front
of THE MODERN MARVELS PAVILION.

STEVE
What'd you tell her about me?

Bucky grins, still waving.

BUCKY
Only the good stuff.

17 INT. MARVELS PAVILION - NIGHT

EXHIBITS LINE THE HALL. A GLASS BOX holds A RED-
SUITED ANDROID.

"DR. PHINEAS HORTON PRESENTS...THE SYNTHETIC
MAN!"
A FIRE EXTINGUISHER rests at the base.
Bucky and the two girls (CONNIE and BONNIE)
hurry past the exhibit. Steve tags after,
ignored.

CONNIE
Oh my God, there he is!

The girls squeal, urging Bucky towards:

18 INT. MARVELS PAVILION, STARK STAGE - NIGHT

A crowd gathers by a stage: "STARK INDUSTRIES
PRESENTS..."
Steve buys PEANUTS as Bucky and the girls get in
close.
On stage, a dashing HOWARD STARK stands with A
1942 CADILLAC.
The girls giggle, smitten.

> HOWARD STARK
> Ladies, you know how hard it can be putting
> on makeup in a car that's bouncing like a
> kangaroo on a trampoline.

Steve offers Bonnie a peanut. She looks at them
with scorn.

> HOWARD STARK (CONT'D)
> What if I told you that in just a few short
> years, your automobile wouldn't touch the
> ground at all?

Stark hits a button. THE CADILLAC RISES, LEAVING
ITS TIRES ON THE GROUND, BULKY DEVICES WHERE THE
WHEELS SHOULD BE.
The crowd gasps. Bucky and Steve gape,
impressed.

> BUCKY
> Ho-ly cow.

> HOWARD STARK
> With Stark Gravitic Reversion Technology
> (patent pending), you'll be able to do
> just tha—

There's a POP and AN EXPLOSION. THE CAR SLAMS TO
THE STAGE.

> HOWARD STARK (CONT'D)
> I did say a few years, didn't I?

The audience applauds. As Bonnie swoons over
Howard, Steve looks around, sheepish.
He spots something in the distance.
Bucky wraps his arm around Connie.

> BUCKY
> Hey, Steve. What do you say we treat these
> ladies-

But Steve's gone. In his place, a LITTLE GIRL
digs eagerly into his bag of peanuts.

**19 INT. MARVELS PAVILION, RECRUITMENT CENTER -
NIGHT**

STEVE stares at A MIRRORED BOOTH in front of THE
RECRUITING PAVILION: "YOUR DUTY: TRY IT ON FOR
SIZE!"
A BURLY MAN stands in front of the mirror. He
looks big and heroic in uniform.
Now Steve steps up. In the mirror, he now wears
A G.I. UNIFORM. HIS DISAPPOINTED EYES BARELY SEE
OVER THE COLLAR.
Just then, Bucky clamps a hand on his shoulder.

> BUCKY
> You're kind of missing the point of a
> "double date." Come on, we're gonna get a
> chocolate soda.

> STEVE
> You go ahead.

Nearby we see Dr. Erskine, A TIRED-LOOKING MAN
in his mid-50s, listening in on the argument.

Bucky eyes the recruitment signs.

> BUCKY
> You're really gonna do this now?

                    STEVE
It's a fair. I'm gonna try my luck.

                    BUCKY
As who? "Steve from Ohio"?
They'll catch you. Or worse, they'll
actually take you.

Steve looks at Bucky with a grim smile of
disappointment.

                    STEVE
You don't think I can do it.

                    BUCKY
This isn't some back alley, Steve.
It's a war. Why are you so keen to fight?
There're lots of other important jobs—

                    STEVE
You want me to sit in a factory?
Collect scrap metal in my little red wagon
while the men are laying down their lives?
I can do as well as them and I got no
right to do any less. That's the thing you
don't get, Bucky. It's not about me.

                    BUCKY
Right. 'Cause you've got nothing to prove.

A tense beat passes between them.

                    CONNIE
Hey Sarge, we gettin' sodas?

                    BUCKY
Yeah. We are.

Annoyed, Bucky walks toward Connie. Then, he
stops, torn.

Finally, he turns back to Steve.
Bucky holds out his hand. Steve sees his
friend's genuine worry. He shakes his hand.

> BUCKY (CONT'D)
> Promise me you won't do anything too
> stupid before I get back.

> STEVE
> Remember, when you attack, you run toward
> the enemy.
> ALT. I can't. You're taking all the stupid
> with you.

> BUCKY
> (affectionately)
> You're a punk.

> STEVE
> (affectionately)
> You're a jerk.

A moment, and Bucky turns to go. He spins as he
goes, for a last little wave...

> STEVE (CONT'D)
> Don't win the war till I get there.

And Bucky goes, swooping up Connie under his
arm. Steve turns to the tent.

20 INT. RECRUITMENT PAVILION - NIGHT

A YOUNG DOCTOR rips a blood pressure cuff off
Steve's arm.

> YOUNG DOCTOR
> You can get dressed.

A NURSE ENTERS AND WHISPERS TO THE DOCTOR, WHO
EYES STEVE.

> YOUNG DOCTOR (CONT'D)
> Wait here.

> STEVE
> Am I in trouble?

> YOUNG DOCTOR
> Just wait here.

He and the nurse leave. Steve eyes a POSTER:

"IT IS ILLEGAL TO FALSIFY YOUR ENLISTMENT FORM.
ONLY TRAITORS LIE TO THEIR COUNTRY."

As Steve SCRAMBLES for his shoes...AN MP SLIDES
OPEN THE CURTAIN. STEVE LOOKS UP AT THE TOWERING
SOLDIER.

> STEVE
> I'm in trouble.

DR. ERSKINE enters, wearing a lab coat, looking
at a file.

> DR. ERSKINE
> So, you want to go overseas, kill some
> Nazis?

> STEVE
> Excuse me?

> DR. ERSKINE
> (offers hand)
> I'm Doctor Abraham Erskine. I represent
> the Strategic Scientific Reserve.

                    STEVE
(shaking hands)
Steve Rogers. Where are you from?

                DR. ERSKINE
Queens. 73rd and Utopia Parkway. And before
that, Germany. This troubles you?

Steve considers this, then shrugs.

                DR. ERSKINE (CONT'D)
And where are you from, Mr. Rogers?
Is it New Haven, or Paramus, or...
(reading the file)
Five exams. In five different cities...

                    STEVE
That might not be the right file—

                DR. ERSKINE
It is not the exams I am interested in. It
is the five tries.
(peering at Steve)
You didn't answer my question. You want to
kill Nazis?

                    STEVE
Is this a test?

                DR. ERSKINE
Yes.

                    STEVE
I don't like bullies, Doctor. I don't care
where they're from.

                DR. ERSKINE
There are already plenty of big strapping
men in this war.
What they need now is maybe the "little
guys," yes?

                    STEVE
        Maybe. What do you do, exactly?

                    DR. ERSKINE
        ALT. Let's say I believe there is great
        potential in every human.
        It's just a matter of bringing it to the
        surface.

Erskine lays out Steve's file. He reaches for a
stamp.

                    DR. ERSKINE (CONT'D)
        I can offer you a chance, only a chance.

                    STEVE
        That's all I'm asking for.

                    DR. ERSKINE
        So, really, where is the little guy from?

                    STEVE
        New York City.
        ALT. Brooklyn

STAMP! 1A.

21 EXT. HYDRA HQ - DAY

ESTABLISHING. A guardpost stands atop a SHEER
CLIFF FACE.

                    JOHANN SCHMIDT (O.S.)
        Are you ready, Dr. Zola?

22 INT. HYDRA HQ, SCHMIDT'S OFFICE LAB - DAY

DR. ARNIM ZOLA'S DISTORTED FACE FILLS A MONITOR.

                    DR. ARNIM ZOLA
My machine requires the most delicate
calibration.

PULL BACK to see Zola actually standing across
the room, peering into A CAMERA. The camera is
trained at...
AN EMPTY CRADLE IN THE CENTER OF A COMPLICATED
MACHINE.

                    DR. ARNIM ZOLA
Forgive me if I seem overcautious.

JOHANN SCHMIDT makes adjustments to a conduit
attached to A LARGE BATTERY.

                    JOHANN SCHMIDT
Are you certain the conductors will
withstand the energy surge long enough for
the transference?

                    DR. ARNIM ZOLA
With this...artifact...I am certain of
nothing.

Zola eyes MORE CONDUITS snaking from the battery
to A CRUDE CANNON. A small, WOODEN TARGET
awaits.

                    DR. ARNIM ZOLA (CONT'D)
In fact, I fear this may not work at all.

Schmidt glances at THE CARVED BOX FROM NORWAY on
a table.

                    JOHANN SCHMIDT
Then we have lost only time, Doctor. But
if it does work...

ANCIENT TOMES SPREAD OUT AROUND IT. We can see

images we already know:
A MAMMOTH TREE...A SNAKE HIDDEN IN ITS ROOTS.

          JOHANN SCHMIDT (CONT'D)
      In a matter of minutes, we might control
      the power of the gods.
      Either way...

His eyes flick over another engraving: A GLOWING
CUBE LAYS WASTE TO A HORDE OF BARBARIANS.

          JOHANN SCHMIDT (CONT'D)
      It is a moment of terrible possibility.

SCHMIDT THEN OPENS THE BOX. BLINDING BLUE LIGHT
SHOOTS OUT.
Zola secures his sunglasses.
Schmidt lifts out AN INCREDIBLY BRIGHT OBJECT OF
PURE ENERGY. He rests it in the cradle.
A SMOKED-GLASS SHIELD DROPS DOWN, covering
the chamber. Through the glass, we now see the
outlines of A CUBE.
SCHMIDT TURNS A DIAL. THE CUBE PULSES.
A GAUGE marked "ENERGIENBATTERIE" glows blue,
beginning to rise: 20%...40%...60%...
But the battery remains cold. Dark.

          DR. ARNIM ZOLA
      We are stable at seventy percent.
      Well within safety parameters.

          JOHANN SCHMIDT
      I did not come all this way for safety,
      Doctor.

Schmidt reaches over and TURNS THE DIAL.
80%...90%...

          DR. ARNIM ZOLA
      At those levels the power may be
      uncontroll—

Schmidt cranks the dial. 100%. THE CUBE SURGES.
OTHERWORLDLY POWER BURSTS FROM THE CUBE IN A
BURNING FLASH. IT FLOODS THE CONDUITS, FILLING
THE EMPTY BATTERY WITH BLUE ENERGY. JUST AS IT
APPEARS THE BATTERY WILL BURST...
THE ENERGY FLASHES IN A SWIRLING RUSH OF
LIGHTNING.
SCHMIDT AND ZOLA GAPE AS, WITHIN THE SWIRLING
ENERGY, A BRIEF, OTHERWORLDLY VISION FORMS.
THEN...ZAP. THE VISION WINKS OUT AS A SEARING
BEAM SHOOTS FROM THE GUN, VAPORIZING THE TARGET,
BLASTING A HOLE IN THE WALL BEYOND.
Zola pulls a switch. The cube powers down.
BUT THE BATTERY STILL GLOWS, HUMMING WITH LIFE.
Breathless, Zola looks uneasily to where they saw
the vision.

>   DR. ARNIM ZOLA (CONT'D)
>   Did you see...

But Schmidt just stares at the destruction around
him. He allows himself a smile.

>   JOHANN SCHMIDT
>   Thank you, Doctor. Your designs do not
>   disappoint...

THE CONDUITS, LIKE THE WALL OF THE LAB, LIE IN
RUINS.

>   JOHANN SCHMIDT (CONT'D)
>   Though they may require reinforcement.

Zola takes a reading at a gauge, impressed.

>   DR. ARNIM ZOLA
>   The exchange is stable. Amazing.
>   The energy we've just collected could power
>   a battleship. Ten battleships.
>   (beat)
>   This will change the war.

Schmidt pours himself a whiskey, hand shaking. He drinks.

> JOHANN SCHMIDT
> Doctor Zola. This will change the world.

23 EXT. CAMP LEHIGH, PRACTICE FIELD - DAY

PAN OVER ELEVEN HEALTHY RECRUITS. Then dip to find...STEVE, looking small but DETERMINED IN ARMY GREEN.

> PEGGY CARTER (O.S.)
> Recruits, Attention!

A WOMAN IN A BRITISH ARMY UNIFORM, PEGGY CARTER, STRIDES UP.

> PEGGY CARTER (CONT'D)
> Gentlemen, my name is Agent Carter. I will be supervising your induction today.

She passes out papers and clipboards.

> PEGGY CARTER (CONT'D)
> To begin with, I shall need you to complete this document.

Steve reads it: "LAST WILL AND TESTAMENT." Two guys next to him look at each other nervously. Steve's not fazed.
A MEATY GUY, HODGE, grumbles as he takes his papers...

> HODGE
> What's with the accent, Queen Victoria? I thought I was signing up for the U.S. Army.

> PEGGY CARTER
> What's your name, soldier?

                              HODGE
Gilmore Hodge, your majesty.

                         PEGGY CARTER
Step forward, Hodge.

He does. She indicates where and how he should
stand:

                    PEGGY CARTER (CONT'D)
Right leg forward, arms like so...

                              HODGE
(suggestively)
We gonna rassle? 'Cause I got a few moves
I know you'll like.

She comes close, also putting one leg forward...

                         PEGGY CARTER
Are you familiar with the art of Jiu Jitsu,
wherein your opponent's size and momentum
are used against him?

                              HODGE
No...

She PUNCHES HIM SQUARE IN THE NOSE. He drops in
a heap, eyes watering, a trickle of blood coming
from one nostril.

                         PEGGY CARTER
(casually)
Neither am I.

The men titter. Steve looks especially pleased.

                    COLONEL PHILLIPS (O.S.)
Agent Carter!

The men leap to attention as COLONEL PHILLIPS

APPROACHES, impressive, all military. Erskine
trails behind him.

                    PEGGY CARTER
          Colonel Phillips.

                    COLONEL PHILLIPS
          I see you're breaking in the candidates.
          That's good.
               (to Hodge)
          You. Get over there in that line and stand
          at attention until somebody tells you what
          to do.

Hodge scurries back. Phillips stands before the
men.

                    COLONEL PHILLIPS (CONT'D)
          General Patton has said that "wars are fought
          with weapons and won by men."

Phillips notices the sickly Steve. He scowls at
Erskine.

                    COLONEL PHILLIPS
          We're going to win this war because we
          have the best men... And because they are
          going to get better. Much better.

23A INT. CAMP LEHIGH, BARRACKS - NIGHT

The men are unloading their gear. HODGE puts up
pin-ups of women.

Steve unpacks a stack of well-worn military
books.

                    COLONEL PHILLIPS (O.S.)
          The Strategic Scientific Reserve is an
          Allied effort, made up of the best minds in
          the free world.

24 EXT. CAMP LEHIGH, OBSTACLE COURSE - DAY

Recruits run through AN OBSTACLE COURSE. Steve
struggles, last.
THE RECRUITS SCRAMBLE UP A CARGO NET. STEVE'S
FOOT GETS TANGLED. HODGE CLIMBS OVER HIM,
SMASHING HIS FACE. FROM AN OBSERVATION PLATFORM,
ERSKINE WATCHES as Steve grimaces but hauls
himself up.

> COLONEL PHILLIPS (O.S.)
> Our goal is to create the finest army in
> history. But every army starts with one
> man.

25 EXT. CAMP LEHIGH, OBSTACLE COURSE - DAY

PEGGY CHECKS A STOPWATCH. THE OTHER RECRUITS
WAIT AS...STEVE CRAWLS THROUGH MUD BENEATH A
BARBED-WIRE NET.

> COLONEL PHILLIPS (O.S.)
> By the end of this week, we're going to
> choose that man.

Hodge kicks out a support. THE BARBED WIRE FALLS
ON STEVE.

> COLONEL PHILLIPS (CONT'D)
> He's going to be the first of a new breed
> of super soldiers. And they are personally
> going to escort Adolf Hitler to the gates
> of hell.
> ALT. He's going to be the first of a new
> breed of super soldiers. And together
> they're going to bring a quick end to this
> damn war.

26 OMITTED

27 EXT. CAMP LEHIGH, PRACTICE FIELD - DAY

STEVE STRUGGLES TO DO A PUSH-UP. Peggy paces as
the recruits do calisthenics.

> COLONEL PHILLIPS
> I guess I just don't understand the
> European sense of humor, Doctor.

PHILLIPS AND ERSKINE WALK TOWARD THEM.

> COLONEL PHILLIPS (CONT'D)
> You're not thinking of picking Rogers, are
> you?

> DR. ERSKINE
> I am more than just thinking about it.
> He is the clear choice.

> COLONEL PHILLIPS
> When you invited a ninety-pound asthmatic
> onto my Army base, I let it slide because
> I assumed he'd be useful to you. Like a
> gerbil. I never thought you'd pick him.

They stop near an open TRUCK, A CRATE OF
GRENADES inside.

> COLONEL PHILLIPS (CONT'D)
> You put a needle in that guy's arm, it's
> gonna come out the other side.

They watch Steve struggling to do his push-ups.

> COLONEL PHILLIPS (CONT'D)
> Look at him! He's making me cry.

> DR. ERSKINE
> I am searching for qualities beyond the
> physical.

                    COLONEL PHILLIPS
Do you know how long it took to set up
this project? The groveling I had to do in
front of Senator Brandt's committee?

                    DR. ERSKINE
I'm well aware of your efforts—

                    COLONEL PHILLIPS
Then throw me a bone.

Hodge powers through his push-ups.

                COLONEL PHILLIPS (CONT'D)
Hodge passed every test we gave him.
He's big, he's fast, and he takes orders.
In short, he's a soldier.

                    DR. ERSKINE
He's a bully.

Phillips stares at Erskine a long moment. Then
he reaches for the CRATE IN THE TRUCK.

                    COLONEL PHILLIPS
You don't win wars with niceness, Doctor.
(grabbing A GRENADE)
You win them with guts.

HE PULLS THE PIN AND HURLS THE GRENADE.

                COLONEL PHILLIPS (CONT'D)
        GRENADE!

It tumbles in the grass, stopping in front of
the recruits.
Steve's eyes go wide.
The rest of the recruits scramble away. HODGE
YELPS. HE THROWS HIMSELF UNDERNEATH A NEARBY
JEEP.

PEGGY MAKES FOR THE GRENADE, BUT STEVE GETS
THERE FIRST, THROWING HIMSELF ON IT.

> STEVE
>
> Everybody DOWN!

Steve waits for the explosion...BUT NOTHING
HAPPENS. After a moment, he opens his eyes,
confused.
At the truck, Phillips just glares.

PAN TO THE CRATE, WHICH WE SEE IS CLEARLY
LABELED: "M-56 TRAINING GRENADES — INERT."
Erskine smiles at Phillips.
Hodge peeks out from under the jeep, SHAMED.

WIDE ON: STEVE, still splayed over the inert
grenade.

> STEVE (CONT'D)
>
> Uh...is this a test?

28 INT. CAMP LEHIGH, BARRACKS - NIGHT

Steve sits alone on his bunk. Around him, eleven
other bunks lie stripped, their footlockers
empty.
DR. ERSKINE enters, carrying a bottle of
Schnapps.

> DR. ERSKINE
>
> Can't sleep?

> STEVE
>
> Got the jitters, I guess.

Erskine indicates his bottle.

> DR. ERSKINE
>
> Me, too.

                    STEVE
Can I ask you a question?

                    DR. ERSKINE
Just one?

                    STEVE
Why me?

Erskine considers this. Then he sighs and pulls
up a chair.

                    DR. ERSKINE
I suppose that is the only question that
matters.

He motions for Steve to grab a couple of water
glasses. He holds up the bottle

                    DR. ERSKINE (CONT'D)
Made in Augsburg. My city. So many forget
that the first country the Nazis invaded
was their own.
(off Steve's look)
I don't excuse what my people have become.
After the first war, my people struggled...
they felt weak, small. Then Hitler comes
with the big show, the marching. He finds
me. Hears of my work. You, he says, will
make us strong.

29 INT. RESEARCH LAB, BERLIN 1938 - FLASHBACK

FLASH: A SLIGHTLY YOUNGER ERSKINE WORKS IN A
BERLIN LAB, WITH JOHANN SCHMIDT, WHO WEARS A
NAZI ARMBAND.

                    DR. ERSKINE (V.O.)
I am not interested. He sends the head of
Hydra, his research division. A brilliant
scientist named Johann Schmidt. Schmidt was

a member of the inner circle, ambitious,
obsessed with occult power and Teutonic
myth. He and Hitler shared a passion for
violence and Wagner.

29A INT. CAMP LEHIGH, BARRACKS - NIGHT

Erskine sees Steve's blank look. Wagner?

> DR. ERSKINE
> German operas about war and heroes. Blood
> and race. Gods afoot upon the earth.
> (shaking his head)
> Me, I like a little Benny Goodman.
> ALT. Me, I like jazz.

Steve smiles. Erskine goes on.

> DR. ERSKINE (CONT'D)
> Hitler uses these fantasies to inspire
> his followers. But Schmidt...he does not
> believe it is fantasy. For him, it is
> real.

29B INT. RESEARCH LAB, BERLIN 1938 - FLASHBACK

FLASH: SCHMIDT PERUSES AN ANCIENT TOME.

> DR. ERSKINE
> He became convinced that a great power had
> been hidden on earth left here by the gods
> —waiting to be seized by a superior man.

FLASH: HE TALKS TO ERSKINE, WHO SHAKES HIS HEAD.

> DR. ERSKINE (CONT'D)
> And when he understood what my formula
> could do, Schmidt could not resist...

FLASH: SCHMIDT, NOW IN A FULL NAZI UNIFORM,
PRESSES A LUGER BETWEEN ERSKINE'S EYES.

DR. ERSKINE (V.O.) (CONT'D)
He had to become that superior man.

30 INT. CAMP LEHIGH, BARRACKS - NIGHT

Erskine goes silent. He just stares at his
hands.

STEVE
Did it make him strong?

DR. ERSKINE
Yes, but there were other...effects.

31 INT. RESEARCH LAB, BERLIN 1938 - FLASHBACK

FLASH: SCHMIDT LIES ON AN EXAM TABLE, SLEEVES
ROLLED UP.

DR. ERSKINE (V.O.)
The serum was not ready, but more
important, the man...

FLASH: ANOTHER NAZI POINTS A GUN. ERSKINE
HESITATES. SCHMIDT YANKS THE NEEDLE FROM HIM AND
INJECTS HIMSELF.

DR. ERSKINE (V.O.)
The serum amplifies what is inside.

FLASH: SCHMIDT'S EYES BULGE.

DR. ERSKINE (V.O.)
Good becomes great...

FLASH: HIS SKIN BURNS. HE SCREAMS.

DR. ERSKINE (V.O.)
Bad becomes worse.

OMITTED

33 INT. CAMP LEHIGH, BARRACKS - NIGHT

Erskine pours schnapps into the two glasses
Steve holds.

> DR. ERSKINE
> This is why you were chosen. A strong man,
> he might lose respect for power if he has
> had it all his life. But a weak man knows
> the value of strength...and compassion.

> STEVE
> Thanks. I think.

Erskine chuckles and puts his glasses on.

> DR. ERSKINE
> Whatever happens tomorrow, promise me
> you'll stay who you are. Not a perfect
> soldier...

HE TAPS STEVE'S CHEST WITH ONE FINGER, LOOKING
INTO HIS EYES.

> DR. ERSKINE (CONT'D)
> But a good man.

Steve clinks his glass with Erskine's.

> STEVE
> To the little guys.

They move to drink, but Erskine remembers
something and grabs Steve's glass before he can
take a sip.

> DR. ERSKINE
> What am I doing, you have procedure
> tomorrow. No fluids.

                    STEVE
          We'll drink it after.

He pours Steve's drink into his.

                    DR. ERSKINE
          I don't have procedure tomorrow.
          (taking a sip)
          Is very good. I save you a little.

34 EXT. HYDRA HQ - DAY

WE HEAR THE OVERTURE FROM WAGNER'S "DAS
REINGOLD."
PAN DOWN THE CLIFFSIDE TO A BIG BAY WINDOW IN
THE ROCK.
Through the glass, we see AN ARTIST PAINTING AT
AN EASEL.
We hear a knocking.

                    DR. ARNIM ZOLA (O.S.)
          Sir?

**35 INT. HYDRA HQ, SCHMIDT'S OFFICE LAB -
CONTINUOUS**

A RECORD SPINS ON A PHONOGRAPH.
DR. ZOLA HESITANTLY ENTERS THE OFFICE LAB AND
STOPS...

                    JOHANN SCHMIDT (O.S.)
          Don't stare, Doctor.

AN ARTIST PAINTS SCHMIDT'S PORTRAIT, PALETTE ALL
SHADES OF RED.

                    JOHANN SCHMIDT (O.S.) (CONT'D)
          Is it something in particular?

                    DR. ARNIM ZOLA
          I understand you've found him.

                    JOHANN SCHMIDT (O.S.)
          See for yourself.

On the table, Zola finds...SURVEILLANCE SHOTS OF
ERSKINE IN NEW YORK: in a cab, buying a hot dog,
being escorted by MP's.
Zola looks up at...Johann Schmidt standing
silhouetted in front of the window. We can't
make out his face.

                    JOHANN SCHMIDT (CONT'D)
          You disapprove.

                    DR. ARNIM ZOLA
          Berlin doesn't feel this is a proper use
          of their resources.

                    JOHANN SCHMIDT
          And you are now their loyal servant?
               (beat)
          Berlin, if they care, can discuss it with
          me personally.

                    DR. ARNIM ZOLA
          I just don't see why you need concern
          yourself. I can't imagine he'll succeed—
               (catching himself)
          Again.

                    JOHANN SCHMIDT
          His serum is the Allies' only defense
          against the power we now possess. If we
          take it away, our victory is assured.

Zola nods, resigned.

                    DR. ARNIM ZOLA
          Shall I give the order?

> JOHANN SCHMIDT
> It's already been given.

Zola smiles tightly and heads for the door.
Then...

> JOHANN SCHMIDT (CONT'D)
> Dr. Zola? What do you think?

Zola glances at the artist, who looks queasy and
frightened.
Zola peeks at the painting (which we do not
see).

> DR. ARNIM ZOLA
> A masterpiece.

36 EXT. BROOKLYN STREET - DAY

Kids scramble out of the street as A BLACK SEDAN
PASSES.

37 INT. BLACK SEDAN - DAY

Steve rides with Peggy, staring out at the
familiar streets.

> STEVE
> I know this neighborhood. I got beat up
> in that alley...and that vacant lot...and
> behind that diner.

> PEGGY CARTER
> Did you have something against running
> away?

> STEVE
> You start running, they'll never let you
> stop. You stand up, you push back... they
> can only tell you "no" for so long, right?

> **PEGGY CARTER**
> I know a bit what that's like. To have every door shut in your face.

> **STEVE**
> Who'd shut a door on you?
> I figure guys would be climbing over each other to hold them open.

> **PEGGY CARTER**
> Depends which door you're trying to go through.

> **STEVE**
> I guess I don't know why a beautiful... agent...why would she want to join the army anyhow? She could do whatever she wanted.

> **PEGGY CARTER**
> You don't know an awful lot about women, do you?

> **STEVE**
> (seemingly smooth)
> You got me all wrong, Agent Carter.
> I don't know anything about women.
> (beat)
> This is probably the longest conversation I've ever had with one.

She is laughing just the teeniest bit.

> **STEVE (CONT'D)**
> I wish I were kidding. Think about it; I don't have any money, so I can't take them to dinner. I'm...kinda short. That doesn't help. Ever. And I don't dance, so that's off the table.

> **PEGGY CARTER**
> You must have at least danced.

                    STEVE
Standing on my mom's feet when I was
seven. I don't know. Asking a girl to dance
seemed so terrifying, and then in the last
few years it didn't seem so important. I
figure I might as well wait.

                    PEGGY CARTER
     For what?

He shrugs, looking out the window.

                    STEVE
     The right partner.

He doesn't see that this affects her. The car
slows.

                    PEGGY CARTER
     This is it.

38 EXT. BROOKLYN STREET - DAY

The sedan pulls up to an ANTIQUE STORE. TWO BUMS
LOLL NEAR THE ENTRANCE. TWO MEN IN SUITS stand
near a row of cars. Steve climbs out, confused.

                    STEVE
     Why did we stop here?

                    PEGGY CARTER
     I love a bargain.
     ALT. I'm redecorating.

39 INT. ANTIQUE STORE - DAY

The bell over the door rings. THE ANTIQUE STORE
OWNER nods at Peggy and Steve.

                    ANTIQUE STORE OWNER
     Lovely weather this morning, isn't it?

> PEGGY CARTER
> Yes, but I always carry an umbrella.

> ANTIQUE STORE OWNER
> I suppose you can't be too careful.

> PEGGY CARTER
> Best to be prepared for a shift in the
> wind.

ALT. (scene):

> ANTIQUE STORE OWNER
> Looking for anything in particular?

> PEGGY CARTER
> A dozen eggs and your finest selection of
> cheese.

> ANTIQUE STORE OWNER
> I'm afraid you'd better try the nearest
> farm.

> PEGGY CARTER
> I buy my milk at the store.

The code exchanged, the woman presses A BUTTON
UNDER THE COUNTER, WHERE A SUBMACHINE GUN hangs
hidden.
Peggy leads Steve through A DOOR IN THE BACK.

40 INT. ANTIQUE STORE, SECURITY FOYER - DAY

They find A MARINE guarding a HUGE METAL DOOR. As
the door whooshes open, the Marine salutes.

41 INT. REBIRTH LAB - DAY

Steve steps out onto a raised platform and gapes:
THE HUGE, ULTRA-MODERN REBIRTH LAB STRETCHES
BENEATH THEM, FAR LARGER THAN THE STORE OUTSIDE.

TECHS OPERATE MACHINERY. ENGINEERS MAN MONITORS.
A FILM CREW SETS UP. They all look respectfully
at Steve.
His eyes alight on...THE REBIRTH DEVICE.
GLITTERING LENSES SURROUND A MAN-SHAPED CRADLE.
PNEUMATIC PANELS FOLD BELOW. SIX VITA-RAY
REACTORS LOOM BEHIND.
Dr. Erskine scurries about in the center of all,
prepping. Steve takes it all in, looking over to
an OBSERVATION BOOTH where a group of men gather.

42 INT. OBSERVATION BOOTH - DAY

SENATOR BRANDT confers with his aides. A man
with glasses waits a little behind. Phillips
enters.

> COLONEL PHILLIPS
> Senator Brandt. Glad you could make it.

> SENATOR BRANDT
> Why exactly am I in Brooklyn?

Phillips looks down to the machines below.

> COLONEL PHILLIPS
> We needed access to the city's power grid.
> Of course, if you'd given us the generator
> I requisitioned...

> SENATOR BRANDT
> Lot of people asking for funds, Colonel.
> (remembering)
> Oh, this is Clem...

The man sticks his hand out as Brandt fumbles
the name.

> HEINZ KRUGER
> Fred Clemson, State Department. If this
> project of yours comes through, we'd like

> to make sure it's used for something—
> (eyeing Brandt)
> Other than headlines.

Phillips nods, as Brandt peers through the window at the lab.
He spots Steve.

> SENATOR BRANDT
> Jeez, somebody get that kid a sandwich.

43 INT. REBIRTH LAB - DAY

Erskine helps Steve onto the device.

> DR. ERSKINE
> Comfortable?

STEVE LOOKS SMALL IN THE OUTLINE OF A MUCH LARGER MAN.

> STEVE
> You save me any of that schnapps?

> DR. ERSKINE
> (wincing)
> Not as much as I should have.

Erskine nods to the attendants, who hook up Steve. He then looks to A MAN IN A SUIT making adjustments.

> DR. ERSKINE (CONT'D)
> How are your levels, Mr. Stark?

The man steps out from behind the device. Steve blinks, surprised: IT'S HOWARD STARK.

> HOWARD STARK
> Coils are at peak, levels are 100%.

We may dim half the lights in Brooklyn, but we're ready. As we'll ever be.

Steve eyes him warily.

                    STEVE
          I saw you at the Expo. Did you ever get
          that Cadillac in the air?

                    HOWARD STARK
          Had her flying three full minutes.

                    STEVE
          Then what happened?

                    HOWARD STARK
          We landed.
              (beat)
          Technically.

He pats Steve on the shoulder. Steve isn't reassured.
Erskine jostles a nervous Peggy as he tries to squeeze past.

                    DR. ERSKINE
          Agent Carter, wouldn't you be more
          comfortable in the booth?

She gets the hint. She smiles at Steve. Steve smiles back.
Erskine pulls down an overhead microphone. He looks to the booth, waiting until Phillips is standing near a speaker. He taps hard on the mic. Phillips winces, holding his ear.

                    DR. ERSKINE (CONT'D)
          Ladies and gentlemen, this morning we do
          not take another step toward annihilation.
          Today, we take the first step on the path to
          peace.

44 INT. OBSERVATION BOOTH - DAY

Brandt watches, skeptical.

> DR. ERSKINE (ON SPEAKER)
> We will begin with a series of micro-
> injections to the subject's major muscle
> groups.

Peggy enters. "Clemson" offers her his seat.

45 INT. REBIRTH LAB - DAY

Stark and HIS OLDER ASSISTANTS ready the
machinery. The engineers check their monitors.
AN EKG BEEPS.

> DR. ERSKINE
> The serum will cause immediate cellular
> change. In order to prevent uncontrolled
> growth, the subject will then be saturated
> with Vita Rays.

He clicks off the microphone and nods to A NURSE.
SHE OPENS A CASE, REVEALING A GLEAMING ALUMINUM
SYRINGE.
She taps the needle, pulls back the plunger...
AND INJECTS STEVE IN THE ARM. He winces...then
relaxes.

> STEVE
> That wasn't so bad.

> DR. ERSKINE
> That was a tetanus shot.

A PANEL SLIDES BACK, REVEALING A CAROUSEL OF
BLUE VIALS. SEVEN TUBES OF SERUM STAND AT THE
READY.
Erskine and the nurse insert SIX VIALS into THE
INJECTORS.

Erskine NODS AT A TECH, WHO DEPLOYS THE
INJECTION PADS. THEY BRISTLE WITH HUNDREDS OF
TINY NEEDLETIPS.
They close over Steve, pressing him to the
table.

> DR. ERSKINE (CONT'D)
> Beginning serum infusion in five, four,
> three, two...one.

He presses a switch. THE INJECTION PADS CLICK.
STEVE JERKS AS UNSEEN NEEDLES DEPLOY.
The blue fluid slowly empties from the serum
injectors. Steve's veins swell. His head begins
to shake.
Erskine hits another button. Padded restraints
close in on Steve's head, holding him still.
Steve's wide eyes glow an intense blue.
Finally, the injector vials empty completely.

> DR. ERSKINE (CONT'D)
> Now, Mr. Stark.

STARK PULLS A LEVER. THE TABLE SLOWLY TILTS
UPRIGHT. STEVE RISES LIKE A ROCKET READY FOR
LAUNCH.
THE PANELS UNFOLD. A HOOD LOWERS OVER STEVE'S
HEAD, SEALING HIM INSIDE THE VITA CHAMBER.
A WINDOW FRAMES STEVE'S FACE. Erskine talks into
a mic.

> DR. ERSKINE (CONT'D)
> Steven, can you hear me?

> STEVE (ON SPEAKER)
> Is it too late to go to the bathroom?

> DR. ERSKINE
> (smiling)
> We shall proceed.

Stark throws a switch. His Vita Ray reactors come online.
Finally, Stark turns the power dial.
A PIERCING WHINE FILLS THE ROOM. ON A HUGE GAUGE, THE NEEDLE BEGINS TO CLIMB.
10, 20...STEVE'S FACE GOES TENSE. INSIDE THE CHAMBER, ORANGE
LIGHT BUILDS IN INTENSITY.
Technicians pull on goggles. Peggy crosses her fingers.
30, 40...STEVE'S EYES SQUEEZE TIGHT AS THE PAIN GROWS.
Erskine checks Steve's vitals. He nods to Stark, who turns the dial higher.
50, 60...STEVE'S HEAD SNAPS BACK, SEIZING.
The EKG beeps faster...and faster...
Peggy stands, worried. Her breath fogs the glass.
70, 80...THE GLOW SURGES, FLOODING THE WINDOW, HIDING STEVE.
The EKG shrieks.
90...A SCREAM ECHOES FROM THE SPEAKER.
Erskine rushes to the window, but can't see in. He barks into the microphone.

                    DR. ERSKINE (CONT'D)
      Steven? STEVEN?

Peggy rushes out of the booth and down the stairs.

                    PEGGY CARTER
      Shut it down!

The light gets brighter. The viewers shield their eyes.

                    DR. ERSKINE
      MR. STARK, KILL THE REACTORS

Suddenly, everyone in the lab hears:

                    STEVE (ON SPEAKER)
     No...

In the booth, Brandt and Phillips exchange an
amazed look.

                    STEVE (CONT'D)
     Don't...

Stark's hand hovers over the dial.

                    STEVE (CONT'D)
     I can do this.

Erskine swallows. With great hesitation, he nods
to Stark.
STARK GIVES THE DIAL A FINAL TURN. 100. THE
WHINE SPLITS THE AIR. THE VITA RAY CHAMBER
FLASHES FROM ORANGE...TO WHITE.
AND THEN IT ALL GOES DARK. THE WHINE DIES. AS
DOES THE EKG.
Erskine goes ashen. Stark stares at his hand on
the dial.
Peggy swallows. Even Phillips looks saddened.
And then...A SOUND RISES: THE STEADY BEEP OF
THE EKG. THE LIGHTS RISE. Erskine hurries to the
device.

                    DR. ERSKINE
     Mr. Stark!

Stark hits a button. The hood and panels
retract, releasing a blast of steam. When it
clears, Erskine can see...
A NEW MAN HANGING IN THE STRAPS. MUSCULAR, TALL,
PERFECT. HIS HEAD RESTS AGAINST HIS CHEST, EYES
CLOSED.

46 INT. OBSERVATION BOOTH - DAY

EVERYONE GASPS AND HURRIES OUT, except THE MAN

WITH GLASSES.
He opens a CIGARETTE CASE and flicks a switch. A
RED LIGHT BLINKS. HE SNAPS IT SHUT AND MAGNETS
IT TO THE CHAIR BOTTOM.

47 INT. REBIRTH LAB - DAY 47

The technicians undo the straps. Steve collapses
into Erskine's arms. The old man staggers.

>   DR. ERSKINE
>   Steven?

>   STEVE
>   Doctor? Did it...?

>   DR. ERSKINE
>   (under the weight)
>   I think... yes...

>   HOWARD STARK
>   (helping him)
>   You did it, Doctor. You really did
>   it.

THE OTHERS RUSH INTO THE LAB. Phillips looks to
Brandt.

>   COLONEL PHILLIPS
>   Sorry you got up early now, Senator?

>   SENATOR BRANDT
>   I can think of some folks in Berlin who
>   are about to get very nervous.

Peggy brings Steve his clothes. He puts on his
old, now much smaller shirt.

>   PEGGY CARTER
>   How do you feel?

Steve groggily looks down at her.

                    STEVE
        Taller...

He pulls on his clothes.

THE MAN WITH GLASSES ENTERS THE LAB. Across the
room, he spies...THE REMAINING TUBE OF UNUSED
SERUM.
He flicks open a lighter, revealing A BUTTON.
Erskine hears the click of the lighter. He
turns.

                    DR. ERSKINE
        Please, do not smoke in here—

ERSKINE SEES THE MAN WITH GLASSES. HE LOOKS
PUZZLED...THEN:
FLASH: KRUGER HOLDS A GUN DURING THE BERLIN
EXPERIMENT.

                    DR. ERSKINE (CONT'D)
        No...

Kruger pushes the button.

48 INT. OBSERVATION BOOTH - DAY

THE CIGARETTE CASE MAKES AN OMINOUS...CLICK.

49 INT. REBIRTH LAB - DAY

The booth EXPLODES, shooting FIRE AND GLASS into
the lab.
Phillips shoves Brandt out of the way. Peggy
pulls a pistol.
ERSKINE sees KRUGER making for the SERUM. He
bolts to get to it first.
KRUGER draws a PISTOL and SHOOTS the old man down.

STEVE
NO!

ERSKINE flies back, SMASHING into the machinery.
KRUGER snatches the last TUBE and races for the
DOOR. PHILLIPS pulls a GUN, winging KRUGER as
he escapes. STEVE bolts to ERSKINE, checking
his wound.

STEVE (CONT'D)
Doc!

Steve cradles Erskine, who stares through BROKEN
GLASSES.
He takes in the result of his efforts. He smiles,
weak but proud. He reaches out...and taps
Steve's chest.
He stops, dead now. Steve stares a moment, then
looks up, filling with quiet rage.

50 INT. ANTIQUE STORE - DAY

Kruger bursts out of the rear door. THE ANTIQUE
LADY PULLS HER SUBMACHINE GUN. KRUGER CUTS HER
DOWN AND GRABS HER GUN.

51 EXT. BROOKLYN STREET - DAY

Kruger races outside to find...THE TWO SUITED MEN
BLOCKING HIS WAY.

HEINZ KRUGER
I have it. Get the car! Schnell!

Kruger and HIS MEN sprint for Brandt's
motorcade.

The two BUMS we saw earlier draw GUNS.

UNDERCOVER BUM
HALT!

They open FIRE, nailing one of Kruger's men.
KRUGER and his remaining man PEEL OUT. The
guards fire, blowing out the car's windows.
Kruger fires the submachine gun out the shattered
window, killing one of the bums.

52 INT. ANTIQUE STORE - DAY

Peggy races for the door just as Kruger drives
past.

53 INT. CAR - DAY

Kruger hits the button on his lighter.

54 EXT. BROOKLYN STREET - DAY

THE MOTORCADE EXPLODES, INCINERATING THE OTHER
BUM.

55 INT. ANTIQUE STORE - DAY

The windows shatter, showering Peggy with glass.

56 EXT. BROOKLYN STREET

Kruger's car speeds away as Peggy rushes into
the street.
She draws a bead on the receding car. BLAM.

57 INT. CAR - DAY

The back window SHATTERS. THE DRIVER'S HEAD
smacks into the steering wheel, a BULLET IN HIS
BRAIN.
Kruger hangs on as he careens toward a parked
car. SMASH.

58 EXT. BROOKLYN STREET - DAY

A TAXI squeals up. THE CAB DRIVER runs to

Kruger's driver.

> CAB DRIVER
> Hey, buddy, are you—

Kruger hauls himself from the wreck and jumps into the cab. The cabbie looks up TO SEE HIS TAXI ROARING AWAY. Gun leveled, Peggy advances down the street. KRUGER aims the cab at PEGGY. SHE stands her ground, squeezing off shots. THE TAXI keeps coming.
Just then, STEVE LEAPS through the FLAMING WRECKAGE and TACKLES Peggy out of the way. The cab fishtails around the bend. Peggy shoves at Steve.

> PEGGY CARTER
> I HAD HIM!

STEVE gets up, BUT falls again, HIS NEW BODY big and awkward. Furious, he takes off after the cab.

59 INT. TAXICAB - DAY

Kruger skids around a corner. The SERUM rolls wildly on the
seat. He snatches it up and sticks it in his front pocket.

60 EXT. BROOKLYN STREET - DAY

Peggy stops A SEDAN. A man rolls down the window.

> DRIVER
> Stay out of the road, there's some—
> HEY!

She yanks him out and gets behind the wheel, peeling out.

61 INT. BROOKLYN ALLEY - DAY

Steve veers down an alley, taking a shortcut.
He spots Kruger's cab racing past the mouth of
the alley. STEVE pours it on, picking up SPEED.

62 EXT. BROOKLYN STREET - DAY

Steve rockets back onto the street, CAREENING
OUT OF CONTROL, right toward a SHOP WINDOW.

63 INT. BROOKLYN SHOP - DAY

STEVE CRASHES through the window, TUMBLING into
the SHOP.

64 EXT. BROOKLYN STREET - DAY

Steve races out the shop door, bare feet
pounding the pavement.
HE passes a speeding CAR.
Kruger swerves past A PARKED TRUCK. Pedestrians
dive away as the cab veers onto the sidewalk.
Steve races between lanes of traffic.
Kruger swerves off the sidewalk, smashing a FIRE
HYDRANT.
Steve follows, tearing down the street, right
at...

65 INT. OLD MAN'S CAR - DAY

AN OLD MAN gapes as Steve runs RIGHT UP his HOOD.

66 EXT. BROOKLYN STREET - DAY

STEVE VAULTS off the car's roof and lands on the
TAXI.

67 INT./EXT. TAXICAB - DAY

KRUGER pulls his gun and BLASTS at STEVE. Steve

ducks, clinging to the side of the car. They
swerve through the streets.
A HORN blares. KRUGER looks to see a TRUCK
ROARING at him. Steve sees the same thing.
Kruger yanks the wheel.
THE TRUCK SIDESWIPES THE TAXI, THROWING it into
a ROLL. KIDS look over from their BALL GAME to
see...
STEVE atop the TUMBLING CAB, riding it like a
rolling LOG.
THE CAR CRASHES TO A STOP.

68 EXT. RIVERSIDE DOCKS - DAY

Steve struggles to his feet.
A BLOODIED KRUGER stumbles out of the wreck,
firing.
ACROSS THE WAY, TOURISTS wait in line for the
STATUE OF LIBERTY FERRY. THEY gape.
A bullet kicks the concrete at Steve's feet.
HE picks up the TORN-OFF TAXI DOOR, holding it
like a SHIELD. ONE TOURIST SNAPS A PHOTO.
Kruger fires at Steve the bullets ripping through
the shield door. SHRAPNEL tears at STEVE but he
just keeps coming.
Finally, KRUGER TURNS AND RUNS.

69 EXT. PIER PARKING LOT - DAY

Kruger shoves through THE PACK OF WAITING
TOURISTS.

                    STRIPED SHIRT KID
          Hey, watch it, mister!

KRUGER grabs the smallest BOY, putting a GUN to
his TEMPLE.
STEVE STOPS. HE LOCKS EYES with the scared,
scrawny KID.

70 EXT. BROOKLYN PIER - DAY

Kruger drags the kid to the water. Steve
follows, relentless.
Kruger points the gun at Steve. CLICK. Empty.
KRUGER hurls the KID in the drink. Steve races
to save him.
Kruger presses his lighter again. A ONE-MAN
SUBMARINE SURFACES. HE SCRAMBLES down to it.
Steve spots THE KID, GRIPPING THE LADDER.

> STRIPED SHIRT KID
> Go get him! I can swim!

Steve spots the departing minisub. He scowls.

> STEVE
> Great. I can't.

71 INT. MINISUB - DAY

THE SUB DIVES, PROPELLERS WHIRRING. Kruger
pilots beneath the hull of a tramp steamer.

72 EXT. BROOKLYN PIER - DAY

Steve sprints the length of the dock and DIVES.

73 INT./EXT. MINISUB - DAY

TORPEDOING INTO THE WATER. Steve kicks for the
sub.
Kruger smiles to himself, pleased at his getaway
until...
WHAM! The sub lurches. Kruger looks behind him
to see STEVE HOLDING ON TO THE TAILFIN.
Kruger pushes the stick, diving. Steve hangs on
tight. HE PUNCHES THE COCKPIT GLASS, AGAIN AND
AGAIN.
STEVE PUNCHES ONE LAST TIME. THE GLASS
SPIDERWEBS AROUND HIS FIST. KRUGER RAGES AS
WATER POURS IN.
Steve tugs on a latch, OPENING THE COCKPIT. He

pulls Kruger out and kicks for the surface.
The sub plows into the silty riverbottom.

74 EXT. BROOKLYN PIER - DAY

Steve throws Kruger to the dock. KRUGER WHIRLS
WITH A KNIFE.
STEVE KICKS HIM. The knife and THE SERUM go
flying.
THE SERUM VIAL SMASHES ON THE DOCK. Kruger
watches THE BLUE LIQUID DRIP THROUGH THE CRACKS.
Steve rolls Kruger over, putting a knee in the
Nazi's chest.

> STEVE
> Who the hell are you?

> HEINZ KRUGER
> The first of many. Cut off one head...

KRUGER PRESSES HIS TONGUE AGAINST A FALSE TOOTH.

> HEINZ KRUGER (CONT'D)
> And two more shall take its place.

HE BITES DOWN ON A CYANIDE PILL.

> HEINZ KRUGER (CONT'D)
> Hail...Hydra...

Steve's eyes go wide as Kruger SEIZES UP AND
DIES.
STEVE LOOKS DOWN AT HIMSELF, STUNNED AT HIS
NEW BODY. He stands alone on the pier, A MAN
TRANSFORMED.
JUST THEN, PEGGY SQUEALS UP IN THE SEDAN. She
jumps out and runs to Steve. More jeeps full of
MP's screech in.

75 INT. HYDRA HQ, CORRIDOR - DAY

THREE NAZI OFFICERS, ROEDER, SCHNEIDER and
HUTTER eye A HYDRA BANNER with distaste as they
stalk after...
Schmidt, who never stops walking.

                    ROEDER
        The Fuhrer feels your continued disregard
        of military protocol is unacceptable.

They pass imposing HYDRA TROOPERS posted along
the hall.

                    SCHNEIDER
        You serve at his pleasure. He gave you this
        facility as a reward for your...injuries.

                    JOHANN SCHMIDT
        Reward? You may call it what it really is—
        an exile. I no longer reflect his image of
        Aryan perfection.

                    ROEDER
        You think this is about appearances? Your
        Hydra division has failed to deliver so
        much as a rifle in over a year. We had to
        learn through local intelligence you had
        mounted a full-scale incursion into Norway.

                    SCHNEIDER
        The Fuhrer feels—how does he put it?—The
        Red Skull has been indulged long enough.

SCHMIDT FINALLY STOPS, TURNS AND GLARES AT
SCHNEIDER.

                    JOHANN SCHMIDT
        You came to see the results of our work.
        Come. Let me show you.

He leads them to a door marked, "ANGEWANDTE IDEE
MECHANIK."

TWO MASSIVE GUARDS stand on either side.

76 INT. HYDRA HQ, SCHMIDT'S OFFICE LAB – CONTINUOUS

Schmidt leads them inside, where...ZOLA AND SEVERAL TECHS WORK ON A BLUE CUBE GENERATOR AMIDST COMPLICATED MACHINERY.

> JOHANN SCHMIDT
> Hitler speaks of a thousand year Reich. Yet he cannot feed his armies for a month. His troops spill blood by the gallon across every field in Europe. Yet he gets no closer to achieving his goals.

> ROEDER
> And I suppose you still aim to win this war through magic?

> JOHANN SCHMIDT
> Science. Though I understand your confusion. Great power has always baffled primitive man.

He gestures to the complicated machinery.

> JOHANN SCHMIDT (CONT'D)
> Hydra has perfected a weapon which can destroy my enemies in one swift, brutal stroke. Wherever they are, no matter how many forces they possess. All in a matter of hours.

> ROEDER
> Your enemies?

Schmidt indicates A MAP MARKED WITH RED PINS.

> JOHANN SCHMIDT
> I now wield enough destructive force to

decimate every hostile capital on earth.
Simultaneously.
Quite simply, gentlemen...I have harnessed
the power of the gods.

The Nazis eye each other.

                    SCHNEIDER
Thank you, Schmidt.

                    JOHANN SCHMIDT
For what?

                    SCHNEIDER
For making it clear how obviously mad you
are.

Hutter studies the map.

                    HUTTER
Berlin is on this map!

Schmidt looks calmly from one Nazi to the other.

                    JOHANN SCHMIDT
So it is.

SCHMIDT PUSHES A SWITCH. A CANNON RISES FROM THE
APPARATUS.
ITS CHAMBER GLOWS A FAMILIAR BLUE.

                    HUTTER
(unaware)
You will be punished for your insolence!

THE DEVICE ROTATES TOWARD THE OFFICERS,
CALIBRATING.

                    HUTTER (CONT'D)
You will be brought before the Fuhrer
himself—

THE CANNON BLOWS HUTTER TO MIST. The other Nazis
scramble.
Schneider jumps away as the cannon fires. It
misses.
Schmidt frowns. He starts to pull his Luger...
Then Schneider trips. The cannon aims again.
BLAM. Roeder backs up toward the wall.

                    ROEDER
        Schmidt!

BLAM. Schmidt gazes down at the dead Nazis,
impassive. He turns to Zola and the Hydra techs,
who stare, shocked.

                 JOHANN SCHMIDT
        My apologies, Doctor, but we both knew
        Hydra could grow no further in Hitler's
        shadow.
        (beat)
        Hail Hydra.

The techs step forward, giving A TWO-ARMED
SALUTE.

                  HYDRA TECHS
        Hail Hydra! Hail Hydra!

Zola carefully considers the moment. Finally, he
relents, offering a measured Hydra salute.

                 DR. ARNIM ZOLA
        Hail Hydra.

76A OMITTED

77 INT. SSR WAREHOUSE, OFFICE - DAY

THROUGH A WINDOW, WE SEE...Howard Stark, in
coveralls and goggles, slowly taking apart the

HYDRA MINISUB.
PULL BACK: Steve stares down at him as AN SSR
DOCTOR AND NURSE draw blood from his arm. Peggy
watches with concern.

                    STEVE
          You think you've got enough?

The nurse fills the vial, resting it beside A
DOZEN OTHERS.

                    PEGGY CARTER
          All of Dr. Erskine's research and equipment
          is gone. Any hope of reproducing the
          program is locked in your genetic code.
          But it would take years.
          (beat)
          At the moment, you're the only super
          soldier there is.

Steve rolls down his sleeve. On the desk he
sees…ERSKINE'S SHATTERED GLASSES.

                    STEVE
          Erskine deserved more than that.

                    PEGGY CARTER
          If it could work only once, he'd be proud
          it was you.

The quiet moment lingers.

78 INT. SSR WAREHOUSE - DAY

Stark works as Phillips enters, Brandt and his
aides on his heels.

                    SENATOR BRANDT
          Colonel Phillips, my committee is demanding
          answers.

                    COLONEL PHILLIPS
          Great. Why don't we start with how a German
          spy got a ride to my secret installation
          in your car?

Brandt frowns, shuts up. Phillips turns to Stark
as Steve and Peggy join them.

                    COLONEL PHILLIPS (CONT'D)
          What've we got?

                    HOWARD STARK
          Well, speaking modestly, I'd say I'm the
          best mechanical engineer in this country...

Stark opens A HATCH. IMPRESSIVE CIRCUITRY blinks
inside.

                    HOWARD STARK (CONT'D)
          And I've got no idea what any of this is
          or how it works. We're nowhere near capable
          of this technology.

                    SENATOR BRANDT
          Then who is?

                    COLONEL PHILLIPS
          Hydra.

Brandt looks at him blankly.

                    COLONEL PHILLIPS (CONT'D)
          I'm sure you've read our briefings.

                    SENATOR BRANDT
          I'm on a number of committees, Colonel.

                    PEGGY CARTER
          Hydra is the Nazi deep science division.
          It's led by Dr. Erskine's first test
          subject, Johann Schmidt.

COLONEL PHILLIPS
Hydra's practically a cult. They worship
Schmidt, think he's invincible.

SENATOR BRANDT
So what are you going to do about it?

COLONEL PHILLIPS
I spoke to the President this morning. As
of today, the SSR's being re-tasked.

PEGGY CARTER
(surprised)
Colonel?

COLONEL PHILLIPS
We're taking the fight to Hydra.
Pack your bags, Agent. You, too, Stark.
The three of us fly to London tonight.

STEVE
Sir? If you're going after Schmidt, I want
in.

COLONEL PHILLIPS
You're an experiment. We're sending you to
Alamagordo.

STEVE
As what, a lab rat? The serum worked!

COLONEL PHILLIPS
I asked for an army. All I got is you. And
you are not enough.

Steve looks sunk. Brandt waves his aide over.

SENATOR BRANDT
With all due respect, Colonel, I think we
may be missing the point.
You've seen Steve here in action. More

importantly, the country's seen it.

Brandt's aide hands over A COPY OF THE NEW YORK
EXAMINER:
"NAZI SABOTEUR FOILED! MYSTERY MAN SAVES
CIVILIANS!"
In the photo, STEVE DEFLECTS GUNFIRE WITH A
STARRED CAR DOOR.

> SENATOR BRANDT (CONT'D)
> Enlistment lines have been around the
> block since this hit the newsstands.
> You don't take a soldier, a symbol, like
> this and hide him in a lab.

Steve looks surprised. He didn't expect Brandt
to step up for him.

Brandt turns on the charm, becoming the
consummate politician.

> SENATOR BRANDT (CONT'D)
> He needs to be out there, showing the world
> what the American fighting man is made of.
> (to Steve)
> Son, do you want to serve your country? On
> the most important battlefield in this war?

> STEVE
> It's all I want.

> SENATOR BRANDT
> Then congratulations. You just got
> promoted.

Off Steve's smile...

79 INT. SMALL THEATER, BACKSTAGE - DAY

CLOSE ON: STEVE'S FACE. He sweats, sick to his
stomach.

                    STEVE
I don't know if I can do this.

BRANDT'S AIDE stands beside him.

               BRANDT'S AIDE
Nothing to it. You sell a few bonds, bonds
buy a few bullets, bullets kill a few Nazis.
Bing bang boom, you're an American hero.

Steve swallows hard.

                    STEVE
Not how I pictured getting there.

               BRANDT'S AIDE
The Senator's got a lot of pull on the Hill.
Play ball with us and you'll be leading your
own platoon in no time.

Steve considers this as A BUGLE PLAYS...

80 INT. SMALL THEATER - DAY

The curtains part. After a long, awkward
moment...
STEVE STUMBLES THROUGH THE CURTAINS, AS IF
SHOVED.
HE WEARS RED BOOTS AND GLOVES, A BLUE COSTUME
WITH A STARS-AND-STRIPES SHIRT AND A MASK WITH
WINGS.
DANCING GIRLS in short skirts look expectant.
Steve stares at the small audience, dismayed. In
the crowd, SENATOR BRANDT LOOKS PLEASED.
Steve glances over his shoulder. Brandt's aide
gives him the thumbs up.
The girls sing, introducing our hero...

               DANCING GIRLS
Who's strong and brave, here to save the
American way?

Steve checks the CUE CARD taped inside his
TRIANGULAR SHIELD.

>   STEVE
>   (hesitant)
>   Who's fighting to keep you safe at home?

>   DANCING GIRLS
>   Who vows to fight like a man for what's
>   right, night and day?

>   STEVE
>   It's the American soldier, that's who.

>   DANCING GIRLS
>   Who will campaign door-to-door for America?
>   Carry the flag shore-to-shore for America?
>   From Hoboken to Spokane, The Star-Spangled
>   man with a plan.

81 MONTAGE.

CITY NAMES SPIRAL PAST as the SONG continues and
the THEATERS get BIGGER...
"BUFFALO." STEVE POSES for a photo with a CRYING
BABY. After the flash...BRANDT'S AIDE hands him
another BABY.
A SIGN READS, "TAKE A SNAP WITH CAP!"
FLASH. Now BRANDT elbows his way in, throwing
his arm around Steve, grinning at the camera.

82 "MILWAUKEE."

STEVE stands in the center of the stage as
DANCING GIRLS circle him, waving tiny FLAGS.

**83 BLACK & WHITE FOOTAGE: STEVE MARCHES with the
TROOPS on a war-torn BATTLEFIELD.**

FADE TO COLOR. Reveal he's marching on a

treadmill on A MOVIE SET. The word "HOLLYWOOD"
spirals up.

84 OMITTED

84A OMITTED

85 OMITTED

85A "KANSAS CITY."

ON STAGE, STEVE takes to the mic, CONFIDENT

> STEVE
> We all know this isn't about having a
> swell afternoon. This is about winning the
> war.

Suddenly, A KID stands up in his seat. Panicked,
he points at "HITLER" CREEPING FROM THE WINGS.
STEVE DOESN'T NOTICE.

> STEVE (CONT'D)
> But we can't do it without bullets and
> bandages. Without tanks and tents. That's
> where you come in.

More kids stand now, shouting. Look out! Behind
you!

> STEVE (CONT'D)
> Each bond you buy protects someone you
> love. So our boys will be armed and ready.

Just then...HITLER RUSHES HIM.

> STEVE (CONT'D)
> And so the Germans will think twice before
> trying to get the drop on us—

STEVE SPINS AND FAKE-SOCKS HITLER ON THE JAW.
THE FUHRER GOES DOWN. THE AUDIENCE GOES WILD.

Steve looks out at the adoring fans, soaking it
all in.

86 OMITTED

A STACK OF CAPTAIN AMERICA #1'S, FEATURING CAP
SOCKING HITLER, THUMPS DOWN AT A NEWSSTAND. 86A

Kids clamor for a copy.

87 "PHILADELPHIA."

IN A LOBBY, KIDS YELL FOR STEVE'S AUTOGRAPH

Steve (IN COSTUME BUT WITH COWL DOWN) hands his
shield to BRANDT'S AIDE.

THE AIDE SAGS under the weight of the heavy
METAL SLAB.

> LITTLE KID
> Hey, Cap, my brother says you took out
> four German tanks all by yourself.

> STEVE
> Sorry, kid. Tell your brother he's wrong...

The kid sags, disappointed. STEVE GRINS.

> STEVE (CONT'D)
> It was eight German tanks.

The kids cheer. A MOVIE MAGAZINE gets shoved in
Steve's face.
Its cover features him: "WHO'S CAP KISSING NOW?"
A smaller photo shows a lonely Howard Stark,
"HAS HOWARD LOST HIS PLAYBOY CROWN?"
Steve looks up to see A BEAUTIFUL BLONDE holding

a pen. She smiles. So does he.

87A "CHICAGO."

CAPTAIN AMERICA BATTLES on a movie screen. STEVE watches from the crowd. He glances around at the RAPT FACES.

88 OMITTED

89 OMITTED

90 OMITTED

90A OMITTED

90B "NEW YORK CITY." RADIO CITY MUSIC HALL.

THREE CHORUS GIRLS sing their hearts out, wearing BLUE HELMETS that spell out "U-S-A."
PULL BACK to see they're sitting on a
MOTORCYCLE...and STEVE is holding that MOTORCYCLE over his HEAD.
REVEAL the wide STAGE of RADIO CITY MUSIC HALL, and a lavish PRODUCTION NUMBER. THE GRAND FINALE.

>   STEVE (O.S.)
>   How many of you are ready to help me sock
>   Old Adolf on the jaw?

91 EXT. U.S. CAMP, MAKESHIFT STAGE - DAY

Steve stands alone on a stage, confident. But instead of applause, he receives...

DEAD SILENCE.

TITLE: "ITALY, OCTOBER 1943 -- FIVE MILES FROM THE FRONT." HUNDREDS OF BATTLE-HARDENED GI'S stare at the man in the red, white and blue pajamas.

> STEVE
> Okay...I'm going to need a volunteer.

> RANDOM G.I. (O.S.)
> I already volunteered. How do you think I got here?

The crowd laughs. Steve stiffens.

> HECKLER (O.S.)
> BRING BACK THE GIRLS!

> STEVE
> I think they only know the one song, but...I'll...see what I can do...

> HECKLER (O.S.)
> You do that, sweetheart!

In the crowd, HODGE nudges the GI next to him.

> HODGE
> Where do they get these guys?

The guy next to him shrugs. THEY BOO. The rest of the crowd joins in.
Steve looks bewildered, trying to keep order.

> STEVE
> Hey, guys, we're all on the same side—

> ANOTHER HECKLER
> Hey Captain, sign this for me!

The guy MOONS him. The GI's laugh. Somebody throws a tomato. Steve has to block it with his shield.

As the chant "Bring back the girls" becomes a roar...

92 EXT. U.S. CAMP, MAKESHIFT STAGE - DAY

RAIN FALLS. STEVE, in an overcoat, sits on the
edge of the stage. He SKETCHES: A CHIMP dressed
as CAP rides a UNICYCLE.

> PEGGY CARTER (O.S.)
> That was quite a performance.

Steve turns to see PEGGY. He stands, surprised.

> STEVE
> Yeah, I...had to improvise a bit. The
> crowds I'm used to are usually more...
> twelve.

> PEGGY CARTER
> I understand you're "America's New Hope."

He sees his CAP SUIT is exposed. He shuts his
coat and sits.

> STEVE
> People buy bonds, bonds buy bullets,
> bullets kill Nazis. Sales rise ten percent
> in every state I visit.

> PEGGY CARTER
> Is that Senator Brandt I hear?

> STEVE
> Hey, Phillips was going to stick me in a
> lab. At least Brandt got me here.

> PEGGY CARTER
> And are those your only options?
> (eyeing his sketch)
> Lab rat or dancing monkey? You know you're
> meant for more than this.

Steve takes this in. Finally...

> STEVE
> It's just, you get enough people telling
> you you're a hero, after years of them
> telling you you're nothing...
> (beat)
> All I dreamed about was coming overseas,
> being on the front lines, serving my
> country. I finally get everything I
> wanted...and I'm wearing tights.

Steve looks up, seeing A PLATOON OF TIRED,
WOUNDED SOLDIERS.
AN AMBULANCE rolls up to the HOSPITAL TENT.
CORPSMEN UNLOAD THE WOUNDED ON STRETCHERS.

> STEVE (CONT'D)
> Looks like they've been through hell.

> PEGGY CARTER
> These men more than most.

Steve eyes her, understanding.

> STEVE
> Hydra?

> PEGGY CARTER
> Not officially.

> STEVE
> Back home, that's a yes.

She considers protocol but leans near him
instead.

> PEGGY CARTER
> Schmidt was moving a force through Azzano.
> 200 hundred men went up against them,
> less than fifty came back. Your audience

contained all that's left of the 107th.
The rest were killed or captured.

>   STEVE
> The 107th?
>   PEGGY CARTER
> Yes, what?

He stands, pulling her up as well.

>   STEVE
> Come on.

93 OMITTED

94 OMITTED

**95 INT. U.S. CAMP, PHILLIPS' TENT - LATE
AFTERNOON**

A CORPORAL types. At a desk across the tent,
COLONEL PHILLIPS signs a stack of letters.
JUST THEN, STEVE BARRELS IN, PEGGY BEHIND.

>   COLONEL PHILLIPS
> Well, if it isn't "the starspangled man
> with a plan." What is your plan exactly?

>   STEVE
> Azzano. I want to see the casualty list.

Phillips points to the RANK INSIGNIA ON HIS
COLLAR.

>   COLONEL PHILLIPS
> You don't get to give me orders, "Captain."

>   STEVE
> I don't need the whole list. Just one name.
> Sergeant James Barnes from the 107th.

                    COLONEL PHILLIPS
          (to Peggy)
          You and I are going to have a conversation
          later that you won't enjoy-

                    STEVE
          Just tell me if he's alive, sir. B—A—R—

                    COLONEL PHILLIPS
          Do not spell at me, son.

PEGGY SEES STEVE'S RESOLVE. SHE TURNS TO
PHILLIPS.

                    PEGGY CARTER
          Sir, Rogers is only on loan to the USO.
          Officially, he is still SSR.

Phillips stares at Steve. Finally, he relents.

                    COLONEL PHILLIPS
          Barnes?

Steve nods. Phillips picks up a thick sheaf of
letters, leafing through the first few.

                    COLONEL PHILLIPS (CONT'D)
          I've signed more condolence letters today
          than I'd care to count. But the name does
          sound familiar. I'm sorry.
          ALT. I've written more letters to more
          mothers than I care to count. I'm sorry. But
          the name does sound familiar.

Steve pales, Phillips' words sinking in.
He stares at A MAP OF AUSTRIA on the wall,
alongside AERIAL PHOTOS OF A FACILITY.

                    STEVE
          What about the others? You're planning a
          rescue mission?

                    COLONEL PHILLIPS
Yeah. It's called "winning the war."

                    STEVE
But if you know where they are—

                    COLONEL PHILLIPS
They're thirty miles behind the lines.
Through some of the most heavily fortified
territory in Europe. We'd lose more men
than we'd save. I don't expect you to
understand that, because you are a chorus
girl.

                    STEVE
I think I understand pretty well.

                    COLONEL PHILLIPS
Then understand it somewhere else. If I
read the posters right, you've got some
place to be in a half-hour.

                    STEVE
Yes, sir. I do.

He exits, taking one last look at the maps as he
goes.

Phillips goes back to signing letters.

                    COLONEL PHILLIPS
(to Peggy)
You got something to say now's the time to
keep it to yourself.

PUSH IN ON PEGGY'S FACE AS SHE CONSIDERS THE
SITUATION.

**96 EXT. U.S. CAMP, MAKESHIFT STAGE, BACKSTAGE -
NIGHT**

Musicians hustle as...BRANDT'S AIDE SEARCHES FOR
STEVE.

>BRANDT'S AIDE
>Where the hell is Rogers? Anyone seen him?

He grabs THE THREE GIRLS FROM THE MOTORCYCLE
NUMBER.

>BRANDT'S AIDE (CONT'D)
>Get out there. Now! Stall!

The first girl hurries to a shelf and grabs her
"U" HELMET.
The second girl grabs her "S" HELMET.
The last girl reaches the shelf to find it...
EMPTY. She looks around for her missing "A"
HELMET.

>"A" DANCER
>ALT. Where's my helmet?

97 EXT. LOCKHEED ELECTRA - NIGHT

A SILVER LOCKHEED ELECTRA CUTS THROUGH THE
CLOUDS.

98 INT. LOCKHEED ELECTRA - NIGHT

THE "A" HELMET from the USO show sits on a
bench. Beside it, Steve buttons FATIGUES over
his Cap shirt.

>PEGGY CARTER (O.S.)
>The Hydra camp is in Krausberg, tucked
>between two mountain ranges. It's a factory
>of some kind.

REVEAL...PEGGY sitting across from him, studying
a map.

HOWARD STARK leans back from the controls.

> HOWARD STARK
> We should be able to drop you right on the
> doorstep.

> STEVE
> Just get me as close as you can.
> (to Peggy)
> You know, you're both going to be in a lot
> of trouble when you land.

> PEGGY CARTER
> And you're not?

> STEVE
> Yeah, but where I'm landing, if anybody
> yells at me, I get to shoot them.

> PEGGY CARTER
> They're undoubtedly going to shoot back.

He shows her HIS SHIELD strapped to his back.

> STEVE
> It's got to be good for something.

> HOWARD STARK
> Agent Carter, if we're not in too much of
> a hurry, I thought we'd stop in Lucerne
> for a late night fondue.

Howard grins. Steve's a little tweaked.

> STEVE
> Why is he saying "fondue" like that?
> What's fondue?

> PEGGY CARTER
> (quietly amused)
> Stark's the best civilian pilot I've

ever seen, and mad enough to brave this
airspace. We're lucky to have him.

                    STEVE
Do you, are you two...fondue?

                PEGGY CARTER
          (all business)
Take this transponder. Activate it when
you're ready and the signal will lead us
right to you.

Steve looks at the insignia, "STARK INDUSTRIES."

                    STEVE
You sure it works?

                HOWARD STARK
It's been tested more than you have.

BAM. THE PLANE LURCHES TO THE LEFT.

99 OMITTED

100 OMITTED

101 EXT. MOUNTAINS - NIGHT

ANTI-AIRCRAFT GUNS HAMMER THE PLANE.

102 INT. LOCKHEED ELECTRA - NIGHT

Howard executes evasive maneuvers.
STEVE straps on his PARACHUTE AND throws open
the JUMP DOOR.

                PEGGY CARTER
Rogers, get back here. We're taking you
all the way in!

EXPLOSIONS ROCK THE AIR. STEVE HESITATES,

REALIZING WHAT HE'S ABOUT TO DO. BAM! HE TURNS
TO PEGGY.

>   STEVE
>   ONCE I'M CLEAR, TURN THIS THING AROUND AND
>   GET OUT OF HERE!

>   PEGGY CARTER
>   YOU CAN'T GIVE ME ORDERS!

>   STEVE
>   THE HELL I CAN'T!
>   (bracing in the doorway)
>   I'M A CAPTAIN!

BAM! The plane lurches once more just as...STEVE
JUMPS.

103 OMITTED

104 INT. LOCKHEED ELECTRA - NIGHT

Peggy catches a glimpse of Steve's chute. She
swears under her breath, then signals Howard,
who hauls on the throttle.

105 OMITTED

106 EXT. HYDRA FACTORY - NIGHT

SEARCHLIGHTS SWEEP FROM WATCHTOWERS. A BARBED-
WIRE FENCE RINGS A COMPOUND OF BUILDINGS. A
FACTORY BELCHES SMOKE.

107 INT. HYDRA FACTORY, FLOOR - NIGHT

A Hydra tech loads BLUE CARTRIDGES into a
CLUSTERBOMB, then gently loads the clusterbomb
into a NOSE CONE.

                    DR. ARNIM ZOLA
          As you see, production is proceeding
          faultlessly.

ZOLA and SCHMIDT walk the factory floor. CATWALKS
RADIATE FROM A CONTROL ROOM OVERHEAD.

                  DR. ARNIM ZOLA (CONT'D)
          Even in ordnance of this size.

                    JOHANN SCHMIDT
          Good. Increase output by sixty percent. See
          to it our other facilities do the same.

                    DR. ARNIM ZOLA
          But our...workers. I am not sure they have
the strength.

P.O.W.'S LABOR AT GUNPOINT. A GIANT CRANE LOADS
BOMBS ONTO A RAIL CAR.

                    JOHANN SCHMIDT
          Then use what strength they have left,
          Doctor. There are always more workers.

108 EXT. HYDRA FACTORY, MAIN GATE - NIGHT

Steve peers out at THE GUARDS PATROLLING THE
MAIN GATE.
He DROPS as headlights sweep the road. THREE
COVERED TRUCKS rumble toward the gate.
A GATE GUARD checks the drivers' papers. In the
background, we spy...STEVE SNEAKING INTO THE
LAST TRUCK.

109 EXT. HYDRA FACTORY, COMPOUND - NIGHT

The trucks roll into the compound, gates closing
behind them.
GUARDS hurry out to unload the trucks. AT THE

LAST TRUCK, ONE GUARD peers in, curious: A
RED, WHITE AND BLUE SHIELD stands amongst the
supplies. WHAM!
THE SHIELD SPRINGS OUT, SMASHING HIM IN THE
FACE.
The guard drops. Steve emerges from the
darkness.

110 EXT. HYDRA FACTORY, COMPOUND - NIGHT

HYDRA GUARDS PROD P.O.W.'S ACROSS THE COMPOUND.
Steve follows, keeping to the shadows.
AT THE BARRACKS, one guard stands watch as the
other leads the prisoners inside...

111 INT. HYDRA FACTORY, BARRACKS - NIGHT

A WARDER opens A CAGE and prods the prisoners
in.
A PRISONER IN A HAT brings up the rear, slow.
THE WARDER hits him with a truncheon, knocking
off his bowler.
The prisoner picks up his hat and puts it back
on. WE NOW SEE IT'S DUM DUM DUGAN. He stares at
the Warder.

> DUM DUM DUGAN
> You know, Fritz, one of these days, I'm
> gonna get my own stick.

The warder viciously kicks Dugan inside. Down
the row, a hundred more prisoners are trapped in
a dozen more cages.

112 EXT. HYDRA FACTORY, COMPOUND - NIGHT

The guard steps out to find HIS PARTNER SLEEPING
AGAINST THE WALL, HELMET OVER HIS EYES.
He kicks him, but the guard doesn't move. He
lifts his partner's helmet to see...HE'S OUT
COLD.

STEVE steps up behind him with a TRUNCHEON.
CRACK!

113 INT. HYDRA FACTORY, BARRACKS - NIGHT

Four prisoners, FALSWORTH, JONES, DERNIER
and DUGAN slump on the floor of their cage,
exhausted.
The WARDER on the upper floor makes his rounds.
He passes out of sight. Then...WHACK!
THE WARDER DROPS on top of the cage,
UNCONSCIOUS. The prisoners jump up as...STEVE
LOOKS DOWN AT THEM.

                 STEVE
   Hi.

The prisoners stare, stunned. Jones raises an
eyebrow at Steve's outfit and shield.

                 JONES
   And who the hell are you supposed to be?

                 STEVE
   I'm...Captain America.

The prisoners' excitement dies.

                 DERNIER
   Merde.

TIME CUT:

114 INT. HYDRA FACTORY, BARRACKS - NIGHT

Freed prisoners follow Steve as he makes his
way down the row, opening cages with THE GUARD'S
KEYS. He releases FALSWORTH, JONES, DERNIER and
DUGAN. Dugan spots A JAPANESE-AMERICAN SOLDIER,
MORITA, already free.

                    DUM DUM DUGAN
What, are we taking everybody?

                      MORITA
I'm from Fresno, Ace.

Steve searches the throng of prisoners.

                      STEVE
Are there any others?

                    FALSWORTH
They did take a number of the men to the
isolation ward. I'm afraid we haven't seen
them since.

Steve considers this as the prisoners gather
round. Finally, he hands them a pistol and
grenades.

                      STEVE
The tree line's northwest, about 80 yards
from the gate. From there, just follow the
creek bed.
(turning to leave)
I'll meet you in the clearing with anybody
I find inside.

Jones stops him.

                      JONES
Wait. You sure you know what you're doing?

                      STEVE
Sure. I've knocked out Adolph Hitler over
200 times.

Steve moves out.

115 OMITTED

116 EXT. HYDRA FACTORY - NIGHT

Steve circles the factory, looking for a way in.

117 INT. HYDRA FACTORY, FLOOR - NIGHT

A HYDRA GUARD stands watch near a door.
He hears...TAPPING. A SILHOUETTE appears behind
the glass. The guard cautiously opens the door
and pokes his head out.

>   HYDRA GUARD
>   Ja?

The door SLAMS, PINNING HIS HEAD. The guard
looks up to see Steve's fist coming right at him.
WHAM!
Steve enters the factory, creeping between bombs
and crates.
Clusters of cartridges bristle inside an
unfinished bomb. STEVE pulls one out, curious. It
GLOWS BLUE IN HIS HAND.
He pockets the cartridge and heads for the
STAIRS.

118 EXT. HALF-TRACK - NIGHT

DUGAN SLAMS A HYDRA GUARD INTO THE GRILL OF A
HALF-TRACK.
DERNIER AND FALSWORTH CLIMB UP TOP. Dernier
settles behind the complicated-looking weapon.

>   FALSWORTH
>   Are you quite sure you know how to use
>   that?

Dernier peers at the grip. BLAM! THE CANNON
DISCHARGES, BLOWING A SMOKING HOLE IN THE
FACTORY WALL.

> DERNIER
>
> Oui.

119 INT. HYDRA FACTORY, CONTROL ROOM - NIGHT

ON A MONITOR, THE FACTORY WALL BURNS.
Schmidt scans his security cameras. He presses a
button, SOUNDING THE ALARM OUTSIDE.
At the controls behind him, Zola looks worried.

120 INT. HYDRA FACTORY, STAIRS - NIGHT

A GUARD rushes down the stairs, his jackboots
almost crushing...STEVE'S FINGERS. STEVE HANGS
UNDER THE STAIRCASE.
Steve yanks the guard's ankle. HE TUMBLES DOWN
THE STAIRS.

121 INT. HYDRA FACTORY, CATWALK - NIGHT

Steve steps onto A CATWALK, only to be met by
ANOTHER GUARD pointing a pistol.
Steve knocks the gun from his hand and smashes
him in the face.
The guard falls, FLIPS BACK UP and charges.
Steve swings from a beam and...KICKS THE GUARD
IN THE CHEST.

122 INT. HALF-TRACK - NIGHT

Dugan stares at the GERMAN CONTROLS, baffled.
Just then, Jones slides into the passenger seat.

> DUM DUM DUGAN
>
> Not exactly a Buick.

> JONES
>
> That one. Zündung.

> DUM DUM DUGAN
>
> You speak German?

                    JONES

Natürlich, natürlich spreche ich Deutsch.
(off Dugan's look)
Three semesters at Howard. Then I switched
to French. Cuter girls.

Dugan pushes ZÜNDUNG. THE HALF-TRACK ROARS TO
LIFE.

                  DUM DUM DUGAN

I didn't ask for a resume.

123 EXT. HALF-TRACK - NIGHT

FALSWORTH AND DERNIER HANG ON AS THE HALF-TRACK
LURCHES FORWARD.

124 INT. HYDRA FACTORY, CATWALK - NIGHT

Steve looks over the factory floor, taking in
the full scale of the bomb-making facility. Just
then... TWO MORE SOLDIERS ATTACK FROM EITHER
SIDE. The first guard fires. Steve drops and
shoots him down. The second guard closes in.
Steve whirls and crushes his neck with the side
of his shield.

125 INT. HYDRA FACTORY, CONTROL ROOM - NIGHT

Schmidt surveys the uprising on his monitors.
OUTSIDE, guards struggle to fend off escaping
P.O.W.'S. INSIDE, a strangely-clad soldier takes
on THREE GUARDS.
Schmidt adjusts his screen: STEVE HITS ONE
GUARD, KICKS ANOTHER, THEN USES HIM TO DEFLECT
THE BLAST OF A THIRD.
MOVE IN ON SCHMIDT'S FACE AS HE STUDIES STEVE,
IMPRESSED.

                JOHANN SCHMIDT

Doctor, prepare to evacuate.

                    DR. ARNIM ZOLA
        I'm sure our forces can handle—

Schmidt eyes Steve on the monitor. Steve
dispatches the last guard and HEADS UP THE
STAIRS.

                    JOHANN SCHMIDT
          Our forces are outmatched.

Schmidt presses a button. ALARMS NOW BLARE
INSIDE THE FACTORY.

ZOLA HURRIES OUT OF THE ROOM. Schmidt flicks the
switches on a line of timers: SELBSTZERSTÖRUNG.
Each of them starts A COUNTDOWN. Then he turns.
THE CUBE PULSES IN A CRADLE BEHIND SMOKED GLASS.
He lowers A TITANIUM CASE over the cradle. It
retracts the cube...PLUNGING the interior of the
FACTORY INTO DARKNESS.

126 EXT. HYDRA FACTORY, COMPOUND - NIGHT
HYDRA GUARDS FILL THE COMPOUND, TAKING ON
P.O.W.'S. MORITA THROWS A GRENADE, BLOWING THE
GUARDS AWAY.

**127 INT. HYDRA FACTORY, ZOLA'S EXPERIMENT ROOM -
NIGHT**

Zola rifles through a filing cabinet in the
corner of a tiled room. He gathers A SHEAF OF
DOCUMENTS.
We glimpse a sketch of a TV-CHESTED ROBOTIC
SUIT.
Beyond Zola, A SHADOWY FIGURE LIES SLUMPED IN A
CAGE.

**128 EXT. HYDRA FACTORY, ZOLA'S EXPERIMENT ROOM,
CORRIDOR - NIGHT**

Steve reaches the corridor. At the far end, ZOLA
SCURRIES OUT
OF HIS ROOM, FILES PRESSED TO HIS CHEST.
Zola sees Steve. Steve advances. Zola runs the
other way.

**129 INT. HYDRA FACTORY, ZOLA'S EXPERIMENT ROOM -
NIGHT**

Steve stalks inside, wary. Past the scattered
files and specimen jars, he sees...THE LARGE CAGE
atop a rusty drain. A PRISONER lies slumped
against the bars. On hearing Steve's footfalls,
he calls out wearily.

PRISONER
Barnes, James Buchanan. Sergeant.
32557038.

Steve gapes, stunned. He can't believe it.

                    STEVE
        Bucky?

Silence. The prisoner doesn't respond. Then:

                    BUCKY
        Who... who is that?

Steve races to the cage. We can now clearly see
a beaten, grizzled BUCKY BARNES staring out.
Bucky squints, unable to focus. He seems to have
aged 10 years.

                  BUCKY (CONT'D)
        Is that...

STEVE SMASHES OFF THE LOCK. HE HOLDS OUT HIS
HAND, GRINNING.

                    STEVE
        It's me, Buck.

Bucky studies his friend's face.

                    BUCKY
        Steve?

                    STEVE
        I thought you were dead.

                    BUCKY
        I thought you were smaller.

Steve gently helps him down from the cage. Bucky
gapes up at his transformed, much taller friend.

                    BUCKY (CONT'D)
        What happened to you?

                    STEVE
        I joined the Army.

130 INT. HYDRA FACTORY, CONTROL ROOM - NIGHT

The first of the timers reaches ZERO. It beeps.

131 INT. HYDRA FACTORY, FLOOR - NIGHT

One of the machines on the factory floor
EXPLODES!

**132 INT. HYDRA FACTORY, ZOLA'S EXPERIMENT ROOM -
NIGHT**

Steve and Bucky stagger as the blast shakes the
room.
As they head out, Steve spots A HUGE MAP,
featuring a series of HYDRA SYMBOLS SPREADING
ACROSS EUROPE.

133 INT. HYDRA FACTORY, CORRIDOR - NIGHT

Steve helps Bucky limp down the corridor. More
bombs go off.

>   BUCKY
>   Did it hurt?

>   STEVE
>   Little bit.

>   BUCKY
>   Is it permanent?

>   STEVE
>   So far.

>   BUCKY
>   You are going to get so many girls.

134 INT. HYDRA FACTORY, STAIRS - NIGHT

Bucky and Steve reach the stairs. They head down,
but ANOTHER EXPLOSION blocks their way.
THEY HEAD BACK UP, SPOTTING A CATWALK HIGH ABOVE.

135 EXT. HYDRA FACTORY, COMPOUND - NIGHT

Morita leads a group of P.O.W.'s toward the main
gate. He hears something roaring up behind them.
He looks.

>   MORITA
>   DOWN!

He tackles a P.O.W. to the ground as...ZAP! A
BLUE BLAST JUST CLEARS THEIR HEADS, BLOWING AWAY
THE MAIN GATE.
Behind THE CANNON, Dernier and Falsworth whoop,
politely.
P.O.W.'S SWARM THE GATE.

136 INT. HYDRA FACTORY, CATWALK - NIGHT

Steve and Bucky reach THE CATWALK only ·to find...
SCHMIDT ON THE OTHER SIDE. Zola waits behind him
at THE ELEVATOR.

> JOHANN SCHMIDT
> Captain America. How exciting.
> (smiles)
> I'm a fan of your films.

Schmidt hands the titanium box to Zola. HE AND
STEVE SLOWLY WALK FORWARD, STUDYING EACH OTHER.

> JOHANN SCHMIDT (CONT'D)
> So, the old man managed it after all. Not
> quite an improvement, but impressive.

STEVE HITS SCHMIDT IN THE JAW, SENDING HIM
REELING.

> STEVE
> You've got no idea.

Schmidt straightens up...STRANGELY PLEASED.

> JOHANN SCHMIDT
> Don't I?

Schmidt swings, but STEVE BLOCKS IT WITH HIS
SHIELD. Schmidt's fist leaves A DENT in the
steel.
Steve gapes, surprised. When he looks up,
SCHMIDT HAMMERS HIM.
STEVE GOES DOWN. Schmidt looms over him.

> STEVE
> (stunned)
> Erskine said your experiment was a failure.

Steve kicks up, driving his feet into Schmidt's jaw. BAM!
SCHMIDT TUMBLES TO THE FLOOR.
Zola scrambles to THE CATWALK CONTROLS. A GAP OPENS BETWEEN SCHMIDT AND STEVE AS BOTH SIDES RETRACT.
SCHMIDT SHOOTS A WITHERING LOOK AT ZOLA. Zola pales.
When Schmidt turns back to Steve...HIS FACE IS ASKEW. RED SKIN BULGES FROM TORN SEAMS.

                    JOHANN SCHMIDT
         A failure? Oh, no, Captain.

He gets to his feet.

                JOHANN SCHMIDT (CONT'D)
         I was his greatest success.

HE PULLS, PEELING HIS FACE FROM THE BONE, revealing...
A RED SKULL UNDERNEATH. HE GRINS, HIDEOUS.
Steve stares in disbelief.

                        BUCKY
         You don't have one of those, do you?

Bucky gapes, then looks at Steve worriedly.

RED SKULL tosses his mask away. JOHANN SCHMIDT'S FACE WAFTS INTO THE FLAMES, STARING AT US AS IT FALLS.

                      RED SKULL
         You're a liar, Captain. You pretend to be
         a simple soldier. But in reality you're
         just afraid to admit we've left humanity
         behind.

ANOTHER EXPLOSION ROCKS THE FLOOR BELOW.

                    RED SKULL (CONT'D)
          Unlike you, I embrace it proudly. Without
          the masquerade...without fear.

                         STEVE
          Then how come you're running?

Steve scowls from the end of the catwalk,
helpless.
Zola hands Skull back his titanium box. Then
the two of them step into the elevator and
disappear.
Steve pulls Bucky away as EXPLOSIONS ROCK THE
CATWALK. THEY SPOT A GANTRY ABOVE.

137 EXT. HYDRA FACTORY, ROOF - NIGHT

Zola eyes Skull's exposed head, queasy. Finally,
he looks away and notices THE FLOOR INDICATOR.

                    DR. ARNIM ZOLA
          Sir? We're going to the roof?

Skull remains silent. The doors open,
revealing...
A CATWALK LEADING TO A WAITING TRIEBFLUGEL...
built for one.

                    DR. ARNIM ZOLA (CONT'D)
          But...what about me?

Skull hands Zola...A SET OF CAR KEYS.

                       RED SKULL
          Not a scratch, Doctor.

Skull exits the elevator. Zola stares at the
keys as the doors close.

138 INT. HYDRA FACTORY, TOP GANTRY - NIGHT

Steve and Bucky reach the gantry. Bucky runs on.
IT CREAKS.
Steve steps on. THE GANTRY DROPS A FOOT. Steve
steps off.

                    STEVE
     Hurry.

Carefully, Bucky limps across the gantry. Rivets
fall.

139 EXT. HYDRA FACTORY, WOODS - NIGHT

Morita leads the injured P.O.W.'s toward the
woods. Just then, SOMETHING ROARS OVERHEAD. He
looks up at...THE TRIEBFLUGEL, its rotating
engines whirling into a blur.

140 INT. TRIEBFLUGEL - NIGHT

Skull glances out the cockpit. Below, his
factory burns. He can just make out...A CAR
speeding down a lonely road.

141 INT. SCHMIDT'S CAR - NIGHT

Files slide on the seat as Zola speeds away. His
feet barely reach the pedals.

142 INT. HYDRA FACTORY, TOP GANTRY - NIGHT

BUCKY JUMPS FROM THE END OF THE GANTRY TO THE
OTHER SIDE.
JUST THEN, ANOTHER BOMB EXPLODES. THE GANTRY
COLLAPSES. Steve stands alone, trapped. Bucky
looks around, frantic.

                    BUCKY
     There's got to be a rope or something—

                    STEVE
        JUST GET OUT!

The explosions come faster now. BOOM! BOOM!
BOOM!

                    BUCKY
        Not without you.

THE ROOF AROUND STEVE FALLS IN. He eyes the
impossible gap.

                    STEVE
        Aw, hell.

He backs up, THEN RACES FOR THE EDGE. Bucky's
eyes go wide as...
STEVE LEAPS, SAILING OVER THE BLAZING CHAOS.
JUST AS THE BIGGEST BOMB YET GOES OFF.
KA...BOOM!

143 INT. U.S. CAMP, PHILLIPS' TENT - DAY

Phillips stares out his window, stoic.

                    COLONEL PHILLIPS
        Senator Brandt, I regret to report that
        Captain Steven G. Rogers went missing
        behind enemy lines on the 3rd of last
        week.

He looks down to read from the rough draft on
his notepad. We see that he's dictating to the
corporal.

                    COLONEL PHILLIPS (CONT'D)
        Aerial reconnaissance has proven
        unfruitful. As a result, I must declare
        Captain Rogers killed in action.

The corporal stops typing. Phillips turns to

see... PEGGY standing in the door, red-eyed and tired.

> PEGGY CARTER
> The last surveillance flight is back.

She enters and lays down AERIAL PICTURES OF THE DISINTEGRATED HYDRA CAMP.

> PEGGY CARTER (CONT'D)
> No sign of activity.

Phillips gazes at the photos. Then he looks to the corporal.

> COLONEL PHILLIPS
> Corporal. Why don't you go get a cup of coffee?

The corporal nods and leaves the room.

> COLONEL PHILLIPS (CONT'D)
> I can't touch Stark. He's a civilian...and the Army's number one weapons contractor. You're neither.

> PEGGY CARTER
> You'll have my resignation in the morning.

> COLONEL PHILLIPS
> I can probably make it so that you'll avoid a court martial.

> PEGGY CARTER
> With respect, sir, I don't regret my actions. And I doubt Captain Rogers did, either.

> COLONEL PHILLIPS
> What makes you think I give a damn about
> your opinions?

Peggy goes cold. Phillips steps forward.

> COLONEL PHILLIPS (CONT'D)
> I took a chance on you, Agent Carter. Now
> that boy—and a lot of other men—are dead,
> because you had a crush.

> PEGGY CARTER
> It wasn't that.
> (quietly)
> I had faith.

> COLONEL PHILLIPS
> Well, I hope that's a great comfort to you
> when they shut this division down.

A commotion builds outside.

> COLONEL PHILLIPS (CONT'D)
> What the hell's going on out there?

SOLDIERS RUNNING BY PHILLIPS' WINDOW. He and
Peggy move closer to look...

144 EXT. U.S. CAMP - DAY

Phillips and Peggy step outside to see DOZENS OF
SOLDIERS HURRYING TOWARD THE CAMP ENTRANCE.
The soldiers part, revealing...
STEVE AND BUCKY WALKING UP THE ROAD, LEADING
A SQUAD OF P.O.W.'S. RAGTAG VEHICLES FOLLOW,
CARRYING THE REST.
Steve's uniform hangs filthy and torn. His shield
is battered and bent. BUT HIS HEAD IS HIGH.
G.I.'s CHEER, more come running.

Hodge steps out of the barracks, drying his hair. He stops, STUNNED.

> HODGE
> Rogers?

Amazed, Phillips looks to Peggy, who wipes away tears. The stunned crowd parts. Steve salutes Phillips.

> STEVE
> Colonel, some of these men need medical attention.

Phillips looks at the gaunt faces of the men. He nods.
Medics rush in to help the P.O.W.'s.

> STEVE (CONT'D)
> I'd like to surrender myself for disciplinary action.

PHILLIPS LOOKS AT STEVE'S BATTERED, BURNED SHIELD.

> COLONEL PHILLIPS
> That won't be necessary.

> STEVE
> Sir, I—

> COLONEL PHILLIPS
> Just how many orders do you plan on disobeying, Captain?

Steve and Phillips lock eyes. Steve smiles.

> STEVE
> Yes, sir.

Phillips turns to Peggy, smiling wryly.

COLONEL PHILLIPS
Faith, huh?

He walks away as Steve turns to Peggy. She stops
herself from hugging him.

PEGGY CARTER
You're late.

He pulls out THE STARK TRANSPONDER. IT'S SHOT TO
PIECES.

STEVE
Sorry, couldn't call my ride.

THEY STARE at each other a long, lingering
MOMENT. THEN...SOLDIERS, including those who
BOOED him at the USO show, crowd around,
slapping STEVE ON THE BACK.
They wave his COMIC BOOK, yelling for CAPTAIN
AMERICA.
FLASHBULBS POP.
STEVE SMILES DESPITE HIMSELF, finally accepted.
A PRETTY NURSE approaches BUCKY.

NURSE
Where do you hurt, soldier?

A SLOW SMILE CREEPS ACROSS HIS FACE.

145 EXT. ALLIED HEADQUARTERS - DAY

BARRAGE BALLOONS fly high over London.
TILT DOWN TO AN IMPOSING BUILDING. A NEWSSTAND
IN FRONT FLOGS A PAPER:
"CAPT. AMERICA TO RECEIVE MEDAL OF HONOR."
TILT DOWN FARTHER, THROUGH THE PAVEMENT TO...

**146 INT. ALLIED HEADQUARTERS, BRIEFING ROOM -
DAY**

A BRIEFING ROOM IN AN UNDERGROUND BUNKER.

                    STEVE (O.S.)
          The fourth one was in Poland, here, not
          far from the Baltic...

Peggy watches STEVE SKETCH PRECISE COORDINATES
ON A MAP, perfectly duplicating the one in the
Hydra factory.

                    STEVE (CONT'D)
          And the last was outside of Strasbourg, say
          thirty, forty miles west of the Maginot
          line.
          (looking up)
          I only got a quick look.

                    PEGGY CARTER
          Nobody's perfect.

An aide picks up the map and carries it across
the room.
Steve and Peggy turn as Howard Stark approaches,
a BLUE HYDRA CARTRIDGE in his hand.

                    HOWARD STARK
          Hey, aren't you supposed to picking up a
          medal right about now?

                    STEVE
          I'm off the publicity circuit.

Just then, Phillips approaches from across the
room.

                    COLONEL PHILLIPS
          Rogers, you just embarrassed a senior
          senator in front of a dozen reporters and
          ten members of Parliament.

He hands Steve a medal.

          COLONEL PHILLIPS (CONT'D)
You should get a medal just for that.

He sees the HYDRA CARTRIDGE.

          COLONEL PHILLIPS (CONT'D)
You figure out what this is, yet?

             HOWARD STARK
If you believe Rogers, it's apparently the
most powerful explosive known to man.

                STEVE
   If?

             HOWARD STARK
Well, either you're wrong or Schmidt's
damn near rewritten the laws of physics.

He moves off toward his lab.

            HOWARD STARK (CONT'D)
And I'm rather fond of the laws of
physics...

Phillips moves toward the room-sized map table.

             COLONEL PHILLIPS
These are all of Hydra's factories.

                STEVE
The ones we know about.
But Sgt. Barnes said Hydra shipped all
the bombs to another facility. And that...
wasn't on the map.

PHILLIPS STUDIES THE MAP, DECIDING. Then walks
toward his office.

> COLONEL PHILLIPS
> Agent Carter, coordinate with MI6. I want
> every Allied eyeball looking for that main
> Hydra base.

> PEGGY CARTER
> What about us?

> COLONEL PHILLIPS
> We're going to light a fire under Johann
> Schmidt's ass.
> (to Steve)
> What do you say, Rogers? It's your map.
> Think you can wipe Hydra off it?

Steve stares, finally given the responsibility
he's wanted.

> STEVE
> I'm going to need a team.

> COLONEL PHILLIPS
> We've already started lining up the best
> men—

> STEVE
> If you don't mind, sir...
> so have I.

147 EXT. THE WHIP & FIDDLE PUB - NIGHT

> DUM DUM DUGAN (O.S.)
> Let me get this straight.

148 INT. THE WHIP & FIDDLE PUB - NIGHT

FALSWORTH, JONES, DERNIER, MORITA, AND DUGAN
lean on stools.
Steve lines up at a DART BOARD.

                         JONES
            We barely got out of there alive and you
            want us to go back?

Steve weighs A DART, then casually tosses a
BULLSEYE.

                         STEVE
            Pretty much.

The men look at each other for a long, pregnant
moment.

                         FALSWORTH
            Sounds rather a good time, actually.

                         MORITA
            I'm in.

Steve eyes Dernier, questioning. Dernier nods.

                         DERNIER
            Je combattrai jusqu'à ce que le dernier
            de ces batârds soit mort, enchainé ou bien
            qu'il pleure comme un nouveau-né!

                         JONES
            (laughing)
            "J'espère touts les trois!"

Dernier laughs, clapping Jones on the shoulder.
When they look up, they see the others not
understanding a word.

                         JONES (CONT'D)
            Oh, uh, we're in.

DUM DUM DUGAN finishes a beer, mustache covered
in foam.

> DUM DUM DUGAN
> I'll fight. Hell, I'll always fight. But you gotta do one thing for me.

> STEVE
> What's that?

He hands over his EMPTY PINT GLASS.

> DUM DUM DUGAN
> Open a tab.

The others LAUGH and hand Steve theirs. Steve grins and takes the glasses back to the bar where...BUCKY WAITS.
Steve slides over the empties.

> STEVE
> Another round?

THE BARTENDER looks impressed.

> BARTENDER
> You drink all these yourself?
> ALT. Where are they putting all this?
> ALT. It is possible to run out you know.

Steve shrugs and turns to Bucky.

> BUCKY
> That was the easiest battle of the war.

> STEVE
> What about you? You gonna follow Captain America into the jaws of death?

> BUCKY
> Hell no. That little guy from Brooklyn who was too dumb to run away from a fight? I'm following him.

Bucky nods at A TOUR POSTER OF CAPTAIN AMERICA: "PERFORMANCE CANCELLED - NOT TO BE RESCHEDULED."

> BUCKY (CONT'D)
> But you're keeping the outfit, right?

> STEVE
> Don't get your hopes up. It's not exactly regulation.

> BUCKY
> I dunno. You saw those guys in Italy when you came back.
> (beat)
> I don't think they were cheering just for you.

The Invaders SING, arms wrapped drunkenly around one another.
One by one, they stop as they notice...
PEGGY ENTERS THE BAR. Out of uniform, she looks great.
Steve is the last to see her.

> PEGGY CARTER (O.S.)
> Captain.

> STEVE
> (standing)
> Agent Carter.

> BUCKY
> Ma'am.

> PEGGY CARTER
> Howard's got some equipment for you to try. Tomorrow morning?

> STEVE
> That sounds fine.

The Invaders start singing again. Terribly.

                    PEGGY CARTER
          I see your crack squad is prepping for
          duty.

                    BUCKY
          You don't like music?

                    PEGGY CARTER
          I do, actually.
          (eyes on Steve)
          I may even, when this is all over, go
          dancing.

Bucky grins and nods at the dance floor.

                    BUCKY
          Then what are we waiting for?

                    PEGGY CARTER
          The right partner.

She smiles at Steve and heads out.

                    PEGGY CARTER (CONT'D)
          08:00, Captain.

                    STEVE
          Yes ma'am. I'll be there.

Bucky stares, puzzled. Steve pats him on the
shoulder.

                    STEVE (CONT'D)
          Maybe she's got a friend.

149 OMITTED

150 OMITTED

151 INT. ALLIED HEADQUARTERS, STARK'S LAB - DAY

ROBOT CLAWS handle THE CUBE CARTRIDGE inside a
blast chamber. Outside, Howard examines it as
HIS ENGINEER takes notes.

> HOWARD STARK
> Emission signature is unusual. Alpha,
> beta and gamma ray neutral. Though I doubt
> Rogers picked up on that.

Howard gently removes A GLOWING PELLET.

> HOWARD STARK (CONT'D)
> Hmm. Looks harmless enough.

Howard steers the robot claw, extending A
SPARKING WIRE.

> HOWARD STARK (CONT'D)
> Hard to see what all the fuss is ab—

He touches the wire to the pellet.
BOOM! AN EXPLOSION BLOWS OUT THE WINDOWS OF THE
BLAST CHAMBER AND SENDS HOWARD SLAMMING AGAINST
THE FAR WALL.
When the dust clears, Howard looks over at his
engineer.

> HOWARD STARK (CONT'D)
> Write that down.

The engineer writes it down.

152 INT. ALLIED HEADQUARTERS - DAY

A PRETTY W.A.C., PVT. LORRAINE, reads STARS &
STRIPES: "P.O.W. CAMP LIBERATED. MIRACLE TREK
ACROSS ENEMY LINES."

                         STEVE (O.S.)
          Excuse me, I was looking for Mr. Stark?

                         PVT. LORRAINE
          (not looking up)
          I think he went to look for a broom.

She looks up. The real-life Steve stands over
her. She slips into a smile.

                    PVT. LORRAINE (CONT'D)
          Of course, you're welcome to wait.

Steve sits, hesitant. LORRAINE SWIVELS IN HER
CHAIR. HE WATCHES HER LEGS CROSS.

                    PVT. LORRAINE (CONT'D)
          I read about what you did.

                         STEVE
          Oh. I was just doing what needed to be
          done.

                         PVT. LORRAINE
          Sounded like more than that. You saved
          nearly two hundred men.

                         STEVE
          Really. It wasn't a big thing.

                         PVT. LORRAINE
          Tell that to their wives.

                         STEVE
          I...don't think they were all married.

                         PVT. LORRAINE
          You're a hero.

DESPITE HIMSELF, STEVE SMILES.

> STEVE
> Well, maybe. Depending on whose definition—

> PVT. LORRAINE
> The women of America owe you their thanks.
> (glancing around)
> And seeing as they're not here...

STEVE'S EYES GO WIDE AS SHE LEANS IN AND KISSES
HIM.
HE STIFFENS...THEN GIVES IN.
When they come up for air...PEGGY STANDS BY THE
DESK.
Lorraine leaps back, flustered. Peggy just stares
coldly.

> PEGGY CARTER
> Captain. We're ready for you...if you're
> not otherwise occupied.

SHE STALKS OUT THE DOOR.

153 INT. ALLIED HEADQUARTERS, HALLWAY – CONTINUOUS

Peggy clicks down the hall.

> STEVE (O.S.)
> Agent Carter. Wait a second.

She doesn't break stride. Steve catches up to
her.

> PEGGY CARTER
> Looks like finding a partner wasn't that
> hard after all.

> STEVE
> Peggy. That wasn't what you thought it
> was.

> PEGGY CARTER
> I don't think anything, Captain. Not one\
> thing.

She continues toward A METAL DOOR at the end of
the hall.

> PEGGY CARTER (CONT'D)
> You wanted to be a soldier. Now you are
> one. Just like all the rest.

Steve stops, flustered and upset.

> STEVE
> Well what about you and Stark? How do I
> know what you two haven't been... fonduing
> the whole time?

Peggy whips around, cold.

> PEGGY CARTER
> You still don't understand a bloody thing
> about women.

She storms down a corridor. Steve watches her
go, at a loss.

> HOWARD STARK (O.S.)
> Fondue's just cheese and bread, my friend.

Steve turns. HOWARD STARK stands in the now-open
metal door.

> HOWARD STARK (CONT'D)
> And it looks to me like she thinks you've
> got a lot more going for you than that.

154 INT. ALLIED HEADQUARTERS, STARK'S LAB - DAY

HOWARD LEADS STEVE ACROSS HIS BRAND NEW LAB.

> HOWARD STARK
> Fondue's just cheese and bread, my friend.

STARK'S TECHS unwrap and install futuristic machines.

> HOWARD STARK (CONT'D)
> And it sounds like she thinks you've got more going for you than that.

WORKERS REPLACE THE BLAST-SHATTERED WINDOWS. Mechanics tuneup A MOTORCYCLE.

> STEVE
> (surprised)
> Really, I didn't think—

> HOWARD STARK
> Nor should you, pal. The minute you think you know what's in a woman's head is the minute your goose is well and truly cooked.

HOWARD STOPS STEVE AT A COLLECTION OF HIGH-TECH FABRICS.

> HOWARD STARK (CONT'D)
> Me, I concentrate on work. Which at the moment is making sure you and your men don't get killed.

He unrolls an impressive gray metallic weave.

> HOWARD STARK (CONT'D)
> Carbon polymer. Ought to hold its own against your average German bayonet. Of course, Hydra's not likely to come at you with a pocket knife...

He turns to Steve's BATTERED SHIELD LYING ON A WORKTABLE.

>   HOWARD STARK (CONT'D)
>   I hear you're sort of attached.

Steve fingers a bullet hole.

>   STEVE
>   It's handier than you might think.

>   HOWARD STARK
>   So's the hotel chambermaid, but I wouldn't
>   take her into battle.

He pulls up a cart with A NUMBER OF SHIELDS,
some built, some half-finished (including the one
from Iron Man 2).

>   HOWARD STARK (CONT'D)
>   I took the liberty of coming up with a few
>   options.
>   (picking one up)
>   This one's fun. It's fitted with
>   transistorized relays.

Steve pulls out A PLAIN, ROUND SHIELD from the
bottom shelf.
He spins it between his palms. It's light,
balanced. Steve pings the simple shield. IT
RINGS LIKE A BELL.

>   STEVE
>   What about this one?

>   HOWARD STARK
>   Oh, that's just a prototype. Now this one—

>   STEVE
>   What's it made of?

>   HOWARD STARK
>   Vibranium. Stronger than steel and a third
>   the weight.

Steve slides the shield onto his arm.

> HOWARD STARK (CONT'D)
> It's completely vibration absorbent. Should
> make a bullet feel like a cotton ball.

BEHIND THEM, PEGGY ENTERS THE LAB.

> STEVE
> How come it's not standard issue?

> HOWARD STARK
> It's the rarest metal on earth. You're
> holding all we've got.

Peggy reaches them, icy.

> PEGGY CARTER
> Are you about finished, Mr. Stark? I'm sure
> the Captain has some unfinished business.

Steve smiles. She doesn't. He lifts the shield.

> STEVE
> What do you think?

PEGGY LOOKS AT HIM, EXPRESSIONLESS.
THEN SHE turns to a table of GUNS, picks one up
and FIRES AT STEVE'S CHEST. BLAM, BLAM, BLAM.
HE BLOCKS them. The slugs FLATTEN AND PLINK to
the ground.

> PEGGY CARTER
> I think it works.

She stalks out of the room.
Steve and Howard WATCH HER GO... FOR A LONG
MOMENT.

> STEVE
> About my uniform...

He hands Howard A SKETCH. NEITHER TAKES HIS EYES
OFF PEGGY.

                    STEVE (CONT'D)
  I had some ideas.

                    HOWARD STARK
  Whatever you want, sport.

CUT TO MONTAGE:

155 INT. HYDRA FACTORY, FRANCE - DAY

A DOOR CRASHES OPEN, REVEALING STEVE DRESSED IN
HIS RED, WHITE AND BLUE BATTLE UNIFORM, FIRING A
TOMMY GUN.
TITLE: "FRANCE, DECEMBER 1943."

BULLETS PING OFF HIS RED, WHITE AND BLUE
VIBRANIUM SHIELD. The Invaders pour in behind
him, blasting away.

**156 INT. ALLIED HEADQUARTERS, BRIEFING ROOM -
DAY**

Peggy replaces an X with an SSR flag on the Hydra
map.

156A EXT. HYDRA FACTORY, BELGIUM - DAY

STEVE AND THE INVADERS FAN OUT ACROSS THE
BLAZING BATTLEGROUND, WREAKING HAVOC.

Title: "BELGIUM, JANUARY 1944."

TIME CUT:
SKULL ROARS UP TO THE RUINED FACTORY IN HIS CAR.
He glares at the destruction as his windshield
reflects the flames.

157 EXT. HYDRA FACTORY, POLAND - DAY

THROUGH A SNIPERSCOPE: Steve stalks a bombed-out
factory.

TITLE: "POLAND, FEBRUARY 1944."

The scope WHIPS to see A HYDRA GUNMAN AIMING AT
STEVE. BLAM. The sniper falls. Steve clocks it
and gives the thumbs up to the camera.
REVERSE: Bucky grins behind his gun.

**158 INT. ALLIED HEADQUARTERS, BRIEFING ROOM -
DAY**

Peggy replaces another X with an SSR flag. She
looks down to the next X, somewhere in POLAND.

159 EXT. HYDRA FACTORY, CZECHOSLOVAKIA - DAY

The Invaders scramble out the side doors of a
HYDRA FACTORY.
They dive for cover and wait.
No explosion. They peer out from their cover.
Where the hell is Steve?
Then...STEVE CRASHES through a factory window on
HIS MOTORCYCLE.
BOOM. THE FACTORY BEHIND HIM EXPLODES.
He hits the ground, roaring toward the camera.

TITLE: "CZECHOSLOVAKIA, AUGUST 1944."

160 OMITTED

161 EXT. FROZEN WOODS - DAY

The woods stand white and silent. Then...
SIX WHITE FIGURES rise out of the snow like
ghosts.
THE INVADERS SHAKE OFF THE SNOW AND CREEP
FORWARD.

THEN A SEVENTH FIGURE RISES: STEVE IN FULL RED,
WHITE AND BLUE.
BLAM! A RIFLE CRACKS, A BULLET PINGS OFF HIS
SHIELD.
Steve spins and hurls his shield...WHUMP. A
HYDRA SNIPER falls out of a far tree.
The Invaders gape.

162 INT. ALLIED HEADQUARTERS, BRIEFING ROOM - DAY

Peggy drops a Hydra flag into a box and pick up
an SSR flag.
She sticks it in the map.

162A EXT. HYDRA FACTORY - DAY

Steve and Jones ride in the back of a jeep as
Dugan drives away from a burning factory.
A HYDRA FIGHTER PLANE swoops over them, guns
blazing.
Steve blocks with his shield as Jones opens up
his .30 CAL.
The plane bears down. Jones stitches it up the
middle. It catches fire, spins out of control...
AND CRASHES AHEAD OF THEM.
Dugan slows to a stop. The three of them stare,
impressed.

162B EXT. FOREST - DAY

Dernier runs through the woods, A BOMB tucked
under his arm.
Parallel to him, a HYDRA FAST-TRACK races along
a road.
Dernier rolls UNDER THE FAST-TRACK. He magnets
the bomb to the bottom of the vehicle as it
roars over him.
He jumps to his feet in time to see the FAST-
TRACK EXPLODE.

163 EXT. BATTLEFIELD - DAY

The Invaders race across a field as...THE
LANDKREUZER BEARS DOWN ON THEM.
They're almost to safety when DUGAN'S HAT FLIES
OFF HIS HEAD, LANDING IN THE PATH OF THE ONCOMING
TANK.
DUGAN RUNS BACK FOR IT. The rest of the men
shout. Stop!
Dugan dives, grabbing the bowler and rolling out
of the way.
He wedges the hat on his head, smug. Then he
realizes the tank has turned...AND IS COMING
RIGHT AT HIM.
Then, from nowhere...
STEVE DIVES OVER DUGAN AND GRABS THE TANK'S
CANNON BARREL.
HE FLIPS HIMSELF INTO THE AIR AND LANDS ATOP THE
TURRET.
Steve spots a GLOWING ENERGY HOUSING, marked:
"EXPLOSIVE!"
He raises his shield high and brings it down.
WHAM! THE TANK GRINDS TO A HALT.
Steve raises his shield again. SMASH! THE HOUSING
CRACKLES.
SPARKS FLY.
Steve brings the shield down one last time. BOOM!
AN OMINOUS DRONE BEGINS TO RISE.
Steve takes a running leap off the tail as...THE
TANK EXPLODES.
FADE TO BLACK AND WHITE. We find we're in...

164 INT. ALLIED HEADQUARTERS, BRIEFING ROOM - DAY

PULL BACK to find Peggy and Phillips watching the
footage.
The camera moves past Falsworth and Dernier
drinking from their canteens. Dugan drinks from a
flask.
Bucky and Steve survey a valley. The camera
focuses on STEVE'S OPEN COMPASS.

Taped to the inside is a NEWSPAPER PHOTOGRAPH...
OF PEGGY.
PEGGY LEANS FORWARD, SHOCKED.
The camera whips up. Steve stares right at us,
pissed. He snaps the compass shut.
Phillips eyes Peggy, amused. She stares at the
screen and...smiles.

SMASH CUT TO:

165 INT. HYDRA FACTORY, GREECE - NIGHT

EXTREME CLOSE ON THE SKULL SCREAMING—a horror-
movie jump from the last image.

          RED SKULL
  YOU ARE FAILING!

Zola cringes before him. Around them, HYDRA
TROOPS SEARCH THE RUBBLE OF ANOTHER RUINED
FACTORY.

        RED SKULL (CONT'D)
  We are close to an offensive that will shake
  the planet, Doctor. Yet we are continually
  delayed because you can't outwit a
  simpleton with a shield!
  ALT. ...a clown dressed in a flag!

Zola gestures at the devastated facility.

        DR. ARNIM ZOLA
  Sir, this is hardly my area of expertise.
  I merely develop the weapons, I cannot fire
  them.
  (beat)
  And the Allies did not take this
  installation easily. Your troops fought to
  the death.

                    RED SKULL
          And now they are dead. I trust you see the
          problem.
               (beat)
          Finish your mission, Doctor.
          Before the American finishes his.

He puts his hands on either side of Zola's head,
squeezing a little, bringing their faces close.

                    RED SKULL (CONT'D)
          You have done great things. Do this one
          more.

Zola contemplates his task.

                    HYDRA SOLDIER
          Sir!

The troops haul the injured PLANT MANAGER, VELT,
from the rubble. Skull bids them forward.

                    MANAGER VELT
          We fought to the last man...

ZOLA CRINGES...as Skull pulls his Luger.

                    RED SKULL
          Very nearly.

Zola turns away, his face illuminated briefly by
AN INEVITABLE FLASH OF BLUE LIGHT.

166 EXT. ALPINE PASS - DAY

CLOSE ON: THE CAPTURED HYDRA CODE TRANSCEIVER.
TITLE: "RUSSIA, JANUARY 1945."
STEVE AND THE INVADERS GATHER ON A HIGH PLATEAU.
Morita crouches over the transceiver. Jones
listens to the transmission. Falsworth wields
binoculars. Dugan and Dernier adjust a winch
at the cliff's edge. Steve and Bucky stand in

conversation we can't hear yet.

                    JONES
          The engineer just radioed ahead. Hydra
          dispatch gave him permission to open the
          throttle.
          (slipping off headphones)
          Whatever's on this train, they must need
          it bad.

                    MORITA
          Well, they're not going to get it.

                    FALSWORTH
          I wouldn't be so sure...

BINOCULAR P.O.V.: in the distance, we can see A
FAR-OFF, SPEEDING TRAIN.

                    FALSWORTH (CONT'D)
          Because they're moving like the devil.

Steve checks his rifle. Bucky looks over THE
CLIFF'S EDGE.

                    BUCKY
          Remember when I made you ride the Cyclone
          at Coney Island?

                    STEVE
          And I threw up?

Bucky looks over the edge again, leery.

                    BUCKY
          This isn't payback, is it?

Steve looks up with a grin.

                    STEVE
          Now why would I do a thing like that?

                    BUCKY
     Jerk.

                    STEVE
     Punk.

A TRAIN WHISTLE SHRIEKS THROUGH THE PASS.
BINOCULAR P.O.V.: A FUTURISTIC HYDRA TRAIN
APPROACHES.

                  FALSWORTH
     All aboard, gentlemen! Mind the gap!

Steve, Bucky and Jones attach T-BARS to the
cable.

                    STEVE
     (to Bucky and Jones)
     Okay, this is a very short, very fast
     train. We've got a ten-second window,
     tops. Mistime it and you're a bug on the
     windshield.

Dugan checks the speed of the train against his
watch.

                 DUM DUM DUGAN
     Better move it, bugs.

STEVE, BUCKY AND JONES HOOK TO THE CABLE
STRETCHING ACROSS THE PASS. Dernier raises his
hand and...DROPS IT.
Steve jumps, shooting away. Jones and Bucky
follow.

167 EXT. HYDRA TRAIN, ROOF - DAY

THE HYDRA TRAIN ROCKETS ALONG.
WHAM, WHAM, WHAM. Steve, Bucky and Jones drop
hard onto the slick roof. They meet eyes: whew.

168 INT. HYDRA TRAIN, REAR CAR - DAY

STEVE KICKS OPEN THE BACK DOOR. He and Bucky
rush in, weapons ready, only to find...NOTHING.
They look at each other. Steve heads for the
next car.

169 EXT. HYDRA TRAIN, ROOF - DAY

ON THE ROOF, Jones crawls toward the engine.

170 INT. HYDRA TRAIN, MIDDLE CAR - DAY

Bucky and Steve bang into the next car...AND
FIND IT EMPTY.

>   BUCKY
>   I thought they were supposed to be hauling
>   something.

Steve unhooks his shield, wary.

>   STEVE
>   They were.

He yanks open the next connecting door, stepping
into...

171 INT. HYDRA TRAIN, FORWARD CAR - DAY

ANOTHER DARKENED CAR. Steve and Bucky creep
forward, then...
WHAM. A STEEL PLATE DROPS OVER THE DOOR, SEALING
THEM IN.
The lights brighten, revealing...A MASSIVE HYDRA
TROOPER.
SIX AND A HALF FEET TALL AND HEAVILY ARMORED,
BOTH OF HIS ARMS SPORT HUGE CANNONS.
STEVE AND BUCKY OPEN FIRE, but their machine gun
bullets ping uselessly off the trooper's armor.

THE TROOPER TAKES AIM AT STEVE...BLAM!
THE BLUE PULSE BLOWS THE SHIELD OUT OF STEVE'S
HAND AND SLAMS HIM INTO THE BACK WALL.
The shield clangs to the floor.
The trooper turns to Bucky and FIRES. Bucky
dives.
THE BLAST RIPS A HOLE IN THE WALL BEHIND THEM.
OUTSIDE, A JAGGED RAVINE WHIPS PAST IN THE
MOONLIGHT.
A RED LIGHT BLINKS FROM A CAMERA ON THE CEILING.

172 INT. HYDRA TRAIN, ENGINEER'S BOOTH - DAY

DR. ZOLA watches on a monitor as the trooper
presses in on Bucky. HE LEANS INTO A MICROPHONE.

> DR. ARNIM ZOLA
> No. Finish the other one.

173 INT. HYDRA TRAIN, FORWARD CAR - DAY

THE TROOPER TURNS BACK TO STEVE as he gets
to his feet. The trooper aims at the star on
Steve's chest.
BUCKY GRABS STEVE'S SHIELD OFF THE FLOOR AND
LEAPS IN FRONT.

> STEVE
> Bucky, no!

BLAM! THE CANNON FIRES, HITTING BUCKY SQUARE IN
THE SHIELD...BLOWING HIM THROUGH THE HOLE IN
THE WALL. WITH A LAST DESPERATE EFFORT, BUCKY
SNAGS THE JAGGED EDGE. THE TROOPER'S WEAPON IS
MOMENTARILY SPENT BY THE BLAST. AS IT STARTS TO
POWER BACK UP...STEVE LUNGES, GRABBING BUCKY'S
SLIPPING HAND. STEVE STARTS PULLING HIM BACK
IN. THEN...BLAM. THE TROOPER FIRES, VAPORIZING
BUCKY'S ARM INTO A BLUE MIST.

174 EXT. HYDRA TRAIN, ROOF - DAY

On the roof, Jones stares in horror as...

BUCKY'S BODY WHIPS AWAY, TUMBLING INTO A
BOTTOMLESS GORGE.

175 INT. HYDRA TRAIN, FORWARD CAR - DAY

Steve reaches out in anguish.

                    STEVE
          BUCKY!

The only response is wind and the clatter of
train wheels.
The trooper takes another step. STEVE GRABS HIS
SHIELD AND TURNS, ENRAGED.
THE TROOPER FIRES. THIS TIME, STEVE HOLDS ON,
KNOCKING THE BLAST AWAY WITH HIS SHIELD. HE
ADVANCES.

176 INT. HYDRA TRAIN, ENGINEER'S BOOTH - DAY

Zola slams his hand on the console.

                    DR. ARNIM ZOLA
          Again! Fire again!

177 INT. HYDRA TRAIN, FORWARD CAR - DAY

THE TROOPER FIRES AGAIN. STEVE DEFLECTS IT AND
KEEPS COMING.
THE TROOPER RE-AIMS. STEVE CHARGES, RED-EYED. HE
THROWS HIS SHIELD AT THE TROOPER.

178 INT. HYDRA TRAIN, ENGINEER'S BOOTH - DAY

THE SCREEN GOES DARK. Zola swallows, frightened.
He turns for the train controls. Then...
CLICK. A .45 PRESSES INTO HIS TEMPLE. JONES HANGS
FROM THE ROOF, GUN ARM EXTENDED INTO THE WINDOW.

>   JONES
>   Stop this goddamned train.

179 OMITTED

180 INT. ALLIED HEADQUARTERS, INTERROGATION CELL - DAY

We see a tabletop and hear a scrape as something is pushed from bottom of frame comes...A PLATE OF STEAK, WITH POTATO AND BROCCOLI ON THE SIDE. Tilt up to see Zola sitting, looking suspicious.

>   DR. ARNIM ZOLA
>   What is this?

REVERSE: Phillips slides over some silverware.

>   COLONEL PHILLIPS
>   It's a steak.

>   DR. ARNIM ZOLA
>   ("I'm on to you")
>   What's in it?

>   COLONEL PHILLIPS
>   Cow? Doctor, do you have any idea how hard
>   it is to get hold of a prime cut like this
>   out here?

>   DR. ARNIM ZOLA
>   I don't eat meat.

>   COLONEL PHILLIPS
>   Ever?

>   DR. ARNIM ZOLA
>   It disagrees with me.

>   COLONEL PHILLIPS
>   How about cyanide? Does that give you a
>   rumbly tummy too?

Phillips slides the plate to his side and cuts
into the meat himself, munching contentedly...

           COLONEL PHILLIPS (CONT'D)
Every Hydra agent we've tried to take
alive has cracked a little tablet before
we could stop them. But not you. So here's
my brilliant theory: you want to live.

           DR. ARNIM ZOLA
Are you trying to intimidate me, Colonel?

           COLONEL PHILLIPS
I bought you dinner!

He slides a piece of paper over to Zola, who
reads aloud:

           DR. ARNIM ZOLA
"Given the valuable information he has
provided, and in exchange for his full
cooperation, Doctor Zola is being remanded
to Switzerland —"

           COLONEL PHILLIPS
Sent that to DC this morning. Of course, it
was encoded—say, you haven't broken those
codes, have you? That'd be awkward...

           DR. ARNIM ZOLA
(not confident)
Schmidt will know this is a lie.

           COLONEL PHILLIPS
He's still gonna kill you. You're a
liability, Doc. You know more about Schmidt
than anyone. Oh, and the last man you cost
us was Captain Rogers' closest friend,

so I wouldn't count on the very best in
protection.
(puts down the utensils)
It's you or him. That's just what she
dealt.

Zola knows he's right. Genuine fear tinges his
response:

                    DR. ARNIM ZOLA
By the time you act, it will be too late.
Schmidt believes he walks in the footsteps
of gods. Only the world itself will satisfy
him.

                    COLONEL PHILLIPS
Huh.
(beat)
You do realize that's nuts, don't you?

                    DR. ARNIM ZOLA
The sanity of the plan is of little
consequence.

                    COLONEL PHILLIPS
And why's that?

                    DR. ARNIM ZOLA
Because he can do it.

                    COLONEL PHILLIPS
What's his target?

Zola just looks at him, incredulous.

                    DR. ARNIM ZOLA
Everywhere.

181 OMITTED

182 INT. THE WHIP & FIDDLE PUB - DAY

Peggy steps through the make-shift door. Steve sips from a beer at the bar.

> STEVE
> Doctor Erskine told me the serum, wouldn't just work on my muscles and my reflexes— he said it would work in my cells, create a protective system of healing, of regenerating. Which means...

He turns to her, somber but clear-eyed...

> STEVE (CONT'D)
> I can't get drunk. Did you know that?

> PEGGY CARTER
> Your metabolism burns three times faster than average. He thought it could be one of the side effects.

> STEVE
> Probably didn't want anybody stealing his schnapps.

> PEGGY CARTER
> It wasn't your fault.

> STEVE
> You read the report?

> PEGGY CARTER
> Yes.

> STEVE
> Then you know that's not true.

> PEGGY CARTER
> You did everything you could—

                 STEVE

I got in over my head. Bucky waded in and
pulled me out, just like he always did.
And the one time he needed me to return
the favor, I couldn't.

            PEGGY CARTER

I doubt it's that simple.

                 STEVE

All I had to do was hold on.

            PEGGY CARTER

Did you believe in your friend? Respect
him?

He looks up at her. Of course.

          PEGGY CARTER (CONT'D)

Then stop blaming yourself. Allow Barnes
the dignity of his choice. He damn well
must have thought you were worth it.

Steve stares at his beer.

                 STEVE

As soon as I finish this, I'm going after
Johann Schmidt. I'm going to burn out
every hole there is for him to hide in.
And I'm not going to stop until he and all
of Hydra are captured or dead.

Peggy nods. Then she takes his beer and drinks
it down.

            PEGGY CARTER

Let's go then.

183 OMITTED

184 INT. ALLIED HEADQUARTERS, BRIEFING ROOM -
DAY

PHILLIPS STANDS AT THE HEAD OF THE TABLE, GRIM.
Steve, Peggy, Howard and the Invaders surround
him.

> COLONEL PHILLIPS
> Johann Schmidt belongs in the bughouse. He
> thinks he's a god and he's going to blow
> up half the world to prove it.

He stabs his finger at A MAP OF THE UNITED
STATES.

> COLONEL PHILLIPS (CONT'D)
> Starting with the U.S.A.

> DUGAN
> That's insane.

> PEGGY CARTER
> So's Hitler, but he's gotten pretty far
> with less than Schmidt has.

> FALSWORTH
> But Hydra would need millions of men,
> fleets of transport. They'd have to be fed,
> fueled—

Howard shakes his head.

> HOWARD STARK
> Schmidt's working with powers beyond our
> capabilities. He gets across the Atlantic,
> he'll wipe out the entire eastern seaboard
> in an hour.

Steve stares at the map, eyes drawn inevitably
to New York.

                    STEVE
Every able-bodied man we have is either
here or in the Pacific. Our borders are
wide open.

                    JONES
How much time have we got?

                COLONEL PHILLIPS
According to my new best friend, under
twenty-four hours.

Dread-filled silence falls over the room.

                    STEVE
Where is he now?

Phillips points to A SPY PHOTO OF A MOUNTAIN.

                COLONEL PHILLIPS
Hydra's last base is here, in the Alps...
        (dragging his finger down)
Five hundred feet below the surface.

Morita gets a closer look at the map.

                    MORITA
What are we supposed to do? It's not like
we can just knock on the front door.

The room goes silent. EVERYONE TURNS TO STEVE.

185 EXT. FOREST - DAY

STEVE BLASTS THROUGH THE FOREST ON HIS
MOTORCYCLE. Trees whip by as he weaves through
the woods. Unwittingly...
HE TRIPS A WIRE ACROSS THE ROAD. A WARNING LIGHT
BLINKS.

185A INT. HYDRA STATION, FOREST - DAY

A hydra scout picks him up on a monitor screen.

185B EXT. HYDRA STATION, FOREST - DAY

HYDRA MOTORCYCLE TROOPERS peel out after Steve.

185C EXT. FOREST - DAY

Steve speeds through the forest. Looking over his
shoulder, he sees TROOPERS SKID ONTO THE PATH
BEHIND HIM.
Steve guns it. But the Hydra riders gain.
Steve eyes the controls on his handlebars. He
hits a button.
The bike's exhaust valve rotates downward: DUST
ON THE ROAD BILLOWS BEHIND HIM.
The first rider gets lost in the cloud. When it
clears...
HE FINDS HE'S HEADING RIGHT FOR A TREE.
BOOM. The bike explodes.
Steve speeds away...but the rest of the pack
keeps coming.
Steve flicks another switch. HOOKS FIRE FROM HIS
SADDLE PACK, embedding in trees on both sides of
the road... STRETCHING A NARROW CABLE BETWEEN
THEM.
Two Hydra riders are plucked off their bikes. The
remaining three duck under the wire and press on.
The lead biker opens fire. Blue bolts explode from
his bike, ricocheting off the shield strapped to
Steve's back. Steve weaves through tight turns...
allowing a Hydra biker to pull alongside.
Steve hits another button...EXTENDING A METAL BAR
BESIDE HIM.
The hydra biker has no time to react as the bar
catches on his front tire...
AND SENDS HIM END OVER END. CRASH!
Steve glances back. TWO BIKERS REMAIN.
Steve opens a valve under his seat, then hits a

red button. FLAMES shoot out from his exhaust
pipe, laying down several yards of fire behind
him.
The nearest Hydra rider is helpless as his
uniform and saddlebags catch fire.
He veers into the woods...and flies off a cliff,
exploding in midair.
One biker remains. He catches Steve on a
straightaway.
He pulls alongside, grinning. He reaches into a
side compartment and pulls a HAND GRENADE...
STEVE SNATCHES IT FROM HIM AND CRACKS THE RIDER
IN THE JAW.
The rider's helmet drops blinding him. He
wobbles...
Steve bites down on the grenade pin and yanks
it out. Then he tosses the grenade back in the
rider's compartment.
Steve throttles up and pulls away, as...
The rider recovers. He lifts his helmet over his
eyes...AND NOTICES THE GRENADE BURNING BESIDE
HIM...
BOOM!

186 INT. HYDRA HQ, HANGAR - DAY

RED SKULL stands beside a HUGE, MYSTERIOUS WHEEL.
He toasts EIGHT PILOTS.

> RED SKULL
> Tomorrow, Hydra will stand master of the
> world, borne to victory on the wings of
> the valkyrie. Our enemies' weapons will be
> powerless against us. If they shoot down
> one plane, hundreds more shall rain fire
> upon them. If they cut off one head...
> (raising his glass)
> Two more shall take its place!

He drinks. His pilots drink.

                    PILOTS
        HAIL HYDRA!

              HYDRA SOLDIERS (O.S.)
        HAIL HYDRA!

Skull turns and only now we see, stretching
before him...

FIVE HUNDRED SOLDIERS IN FORMATION. They salute
in unison.

              HYDRA SOLDIERS (CONT'D)
        HAIL HYDRA! HAIL HYDRA!

As Skull takes in the devotion, he notices A RED
LIGHT FLASHING ON THE WALL. He slowly turns as,
up above...

187 EXT. HYDRA HQ, MOUNTAINTOP - DAY

ALARMS SOUND AT THE SURFACE ENTRANCE. BARBED
WIRE TOPS AN EARTHEN-WALLED COMPOUND.
HYDRA SOLDIERS race to take positions. One
scrambles to look over the wall, only to see...
STEVE SHOOTING RIGHT AT HIM.
THE BIKE RAMPS OFF A GUN EMPLACEMENT, LAUNCHES
THROUGH THE BARBED WIRE AND CRASHES INTO THE
COMPOUND.
STEVE CRUSHES ONE GUARD. WHIPPING WIRE SLASHES
ANOTHER. GUARDS OPEN FIRE. Steve swerves,
tossing a grenade. BOOM!
ONE GUARD LEVELS A BAZOOKA. STEVE RAISES HIS
SHIELD AND DEFLECTS THE BLAST BACK. Finally, a
Hydra rifleman BLOWS OUT STEVE'S TIRE.
STEVE'S FRONT FORK DIGS INTO THE GROUND,
THROWING HIM OVER THE HANDLEBARS.
HE GETS TO HIS FEET, SWINGING, AS DOZENS OF
GUARDS MOVE IN...PUMMELLING HIM FROM ALL SIDES.

188 INT. HYDRA HQ, SCHMIDT'S OFFICE LAB - DAY

Guards drag in Steve. He stares up at Skull's
grotesque portrait. THEN...SKULL STEPS FROM THE
SHADOWS.
Steve struggles. THE GUARDS HOLD HIM TIGHT.

                    RED SKULL (O.S.)
          Arrogance may not be a uniquely American
          trait...but I will say you do it better
          than anyone else.

Skull leans in, TEETH GLEAMING IN HIS CRIMSON
FACE.

                    RED SKULL (CONT'D)
          There are limits to what even you can do,
          Captain. Or did Erskine tell you otherwise?

                    STEVE
          He told me you were insane. That seemed
          like enough.

                    RED SKULL
          He resented my genius and tried to deny me
          what was rightfully mine. Yet he gave you
          everything.
                    (almost wounded)
          What made you so special?

                    STEVE
          Nothing...

He slowly raises his head, staring INTO SKULL'S
SUNKEN EYES.

                    STEVE (CONT'D)
          I'm just a kid from Brooklyn.

Skull seethes.
He SMASHES STEVE IN THE FACE.
The guards grip Steve's arms, holding him up as

the SKULL BATTERS HIM. Again and again.
After a long time, Skull steps back. Steve
pants, beaten, exhausted. Then finally...HE
SMILES.

                    STEVE (CONT'D)
          I can do this all day.

                    RED SKULL
          I believe you can. But I am on a schedule.

He pulls his Luger. Steve stares down the
barrel.

                    STEVE
          So am I.

THUNK. THUNK. THUNK.
Skull turns toward the window to see...THREE
SPECKS IN THE DISTANCE, FLYING STRAIGHT TOWARD
THE GLASS.
Skull spins back to Steve, pistol leveled...ZAP!
STEVE SWINGS A GUARD AROUND, BLOCKING THE BLAST.
THE GUARD IS INCINERATED AS...DUGAN, FALSWORTH,
AND JONES SMASH THROUGH THE WINDOW ON ZIPLINES.
JONES LANDS ON SKULL'S DESK, BLASTING AWAY WITH
HIS .30 CAL.

188A INT. HYDRA HQ, CORRIDOR - DAY

The zipline extends from A POWERFUL GRAPPLING
GUN.
DERNIER hooks to the wire and shoots away.
MORITA barks into his radio.

                    MORITA
          We're in. Go! Go! Go!

188AA EXT. FOREST, RIDGE - DAY

OFF SCREEN, ON A COMBAT RADIO:

> MORITA (ON RADIO)
> Assault team! Go!

ATOP A RIDGE, COLONEL PHILLIPS STANDS.

> COLONEL PHILLIPS
> You heard him! Move out!

PEGGY AND HUNDREDS OF ALLIED TROOPS SLIP OUT OF
HIDING.
Phillips looks to Peggy. He cocks his shotgun.

188B EXT. HYDRA HQ, MOUNTAINTOP - DAY

UP TOP, ALLIED SOLDIERS OPEN FIRE, POURING INTO
THE COMPOUND.

188C INT. HYDRA HQ, SCHMIDT'S OFFICE - DAY

DUGAN LANDS A HAYMAKER. STEVE KNOCKS OUT THE
OTHER GUARD.
SKULL GETS OFF A FEW BLASTS AS HE BACKS OUT THE
DOOR.
DOWN THE HALL, ALLIED SOLDIERS BLOW THROUGH THE
DOUBLE DOORS.
Falsworth cuts down a guard, taking THE SHIELD
from him. He tosses it to Steve.

> STEVE
> Thanks.

> FALSWORTH
> Cheers.

Steve straps on the shield and races after
Skull.

189 INT. HYDRA HQ, CORRIDOR - DAY

FOUR HYDRA TROOPERS back up to the entrance, firing.
BLAM! One falls, shot. A second tries to lob a grenade. BLAM!
He falls, dropping the grenade at the feet of the third. BOOM!
Trapped, the last one panics, TONGUE FUMBLING IN HIS MOUTH.

> HYDRA SOLDIER
> Cut off one head, two more shall rise—

BLAM. The soldier falls dead.
REVERSE: COLONEL PHILLIPS STANDS THERE, SHOTGUN SMOKING.

> COLONEL PHILLIPS
> Let's go find two more.

A DOZEN MARINES FOLLOW HIM INSIDE.

190 INT. HYDRA HQ, CORRIDOR - DAY 190

Skull runs down a corridor, jackboots pounding.
Steve tears after him, racing around the corner, only to be met by a VICIOUS BARRAGE.
Schmidt unloads his Luger, BLASTING BLUE BOLTS.
Steve barely gets his shield up in time.

191 OMITTED

192 INT. HYDRA HQ, CORRIDOR - DAY

Schmidt races PAST AN INTERSECTING CORRIDOR.
He dashes through a doorway and hits a button:
BLAST DOORS BEGIN TO CLOSE.
Steve spots the closing doors. He calculates and HURLS HIS SHIELD. It whirls down the corridor and...THUNK, JAMS BETWEEN THE DOORS, HOLDING

THEM OPEN. Steve takes off after Schmidt...
BUT A HYDRA FLAME TROOPER STOMPS OUT OF THE
INTERSECTING CORRIDOR, BLOCKING HIS WAY. The
flame trooper raises his twin guns. Steve raises
his arm, only to realize...HIS SHIELD IS STUCK
IN THE DOOR. Uh-oh. Blue fire flickers from the
trooper's nozzles. Then...
BLAM! The trooper staggers. THE TANK ON HIS BACK
EXPLODES.
PEGGY steps out of the corridor, RIFLE IN HAND.

                    STEVE
     You're late.

                    PEGGY CARTER
          Tell me you're not complaining.
          (nodding at the door)
          Weren't you about to...?

                    STEVE
     Right.

He sprints for the door, sliding below the
shield, grabbing it as he goes. The doors slam
behind him.
Peggy waves ON A SQUAD OF SSR TROOPS BEHIND HER.

193 INT. HYDRA HQ, CORRIDOR - DAY

DERNIER and FALSWORTH fight along a corridor,
OUTNUMBERED.
Falsworth nods to Dernier. THEY RETREAT around a
bend.
SURPRISED, THE HYDRA TROOPERS GIVE CHASE. After
a moment...THE HYDRA TROOPERS COME RUNNING BACK.
DUGAN STEPS OUT, FIRING A HYDRA CANNON. BLAM!

194 INT. SUBORBITAL BOMBER, COCKPIT - DAY

INSIDE THE BOMBER, DIM MONITORS LINE AN
IMPRESSIVE COCKPIT. A HIGH-TECH CRADLE STANDS IN

THE CENTER.
Skull approaches, carrying the TITANIUM BOX.
He places it over the cradle and dispenses...
THE CUBE. Blue circuits flash. LIGHTS AND GAUGES
FLICKER.

195 INT. HYDRA HQ, CORRIDOR - DAY

Steve runs toward another door. BEYOND, A HUGE
HANGAR LOOMS.
Suddenly, A DEEP RUMBLING SHAKES THE BASE. Steve
gapes.
Through the doorway, he sees...A GIGANTIC PLANE
ROLLS PAST. IT DWARFS ANY WE'VE EVER SEEN.

196 INT. HYDRA HQ, HANGAR - DAY

Steve skids into the hangar. The massive plane
taxies down the runway. In the shadows, FIVE
MORE BOMBERS WAIT.
Schmidt's plane picks up speed. STEVE TAKES OFF
AFTER IT.

197 INT. SUBORBITAL BOMBER, COCKPIT - DAY

Skull throttles up. He presses a button.

198 INT. HYDRA HQ, HANGAR - DAY

At the far end, A DOOR OPENS, letting in THE
GLARE OF DAYLIGHT.
STEVE CHASES AFTER THE PLANE, but the huge
bomber picks up speed. It starts to pull away.
Suddenly, AN ENGINE REVS. SCHMIDT'S CAR comes
up alongside the still-running STEVE, COLONEL
PHILLIPS behind the wheel.

                    COLONEL PHILLIPS
          Get in.

STEVE JUMPS IN without the car ever slowing

down. In the back, PEGGY CHAMBERS A ROUND INTO PHILLIPS' SHOTGUN.

199 INT. SUBORBITAL BOMBER, COCKPIT - DAY

Skull accelerates. On his monitor, he spies... HIS CAR.

200 INT. HYDRA HQ, HANGAR - DAY

Phillips gains on the plane. Just then, the BOMBER'S REAR PROPELLERS SPIN INTO A BLUR. The plane widens the gap. Phillips spots a TOGGLE SWITCH on the dash, "KOMPRESSOR." He hits it. WHOOSH. THE CAR LEAPS FORWARD, THROWING THEM BACK.
Steve climbs over the windshield and steadies himself.

> STEVE
>
> Closer!

Phillips floors it. The car surges toward THE PROPELLERS.
STEVE DROPS just as the propellers SHAVE OFF THE HYDRA HOOD ORNAMENT.
He and Peggy share a worried look.

201 INT. SUBORBITAL BOMBER, COCKPIT - DAY

Skull races for the mouth of the tunnel. On the monitor...

202 INT. HYDRA HQ, HANGAR - DAY

PHILLIPS COMES UP ALONGSIDE THE PLANE'S HUGE TIRE.

> STEVE
> Hold it steady this time.

PEGGY CARTER
Wait!

Peggy grabs Steve by the neck AND KISSES HIM.
When they break off, Steve looks at her, wide-
eyed.

PEGGY CARTER (CONT'D)
Go get him.

Steve nods, stunned. He looks to Phillips.

COLONEL PHILLIPS
I'm not kissing you!

203 INT. SUBORBITAL BOMBER, COCKPIT - DAY

Skull punches the throttle, the SPEEDOMETER RED-
LINING.

204 INT. HYDRA HQ, HANGAR - DAY

Steve braces himself on the hood.
Phillips pulls to within inches of THE SPINNING
WHEEL. JUST THEN...

205 EXT. HYDRA HQ, CLIFF - DAY

THE PLANE BURSTS OUT OF THE TUNNEL.
PHILLIPS SPOTS THE GORGE AHEAD. HE SLAMS ON
THE BRAKES. AT THE LAST MOMENT, STEVE LEAPS...
SNAGGING THE LANDING GEAR. THE PLANE SHOOTS OVER
THE EDGE, SAILING INTO THE AIR.
Phillips skids to a stop. Peggy sees STEVE
HANGING ON.

206 EXT. SUBORBITAL BOMBER, LANDING GEAR - DAY

Steve locks his arm around a strut. THE PLANE
GAINS ALTITUDE. He looks for a way in. Just
then... THE LANDING GEAR GROANS. THE WHEELS

RETRACT. STEVE FINDS
HIMSELF RIDING THE LANDING GEAR RIGHT INTO...

207 INT. SUBORBITAL BOMBER, FLIGHT DECK - DAY

The flight deck. STEVE STARES, AWESTRUCK. He
realizes the propellers are attached to EIGHT
FIGHTERS INSIDE THE WING.
Each features a snub-nose CUBE BOMB as its
nosecone.
ZING. A BULLET RICOCHETS off Steve's shield. He
spins as...
THE EIGHT PILOTS RUSH DOWN A RAMP FROM THE
BRIDGE.
STEVE flips into a flying spin kick, dropping two
pilots where they stand. THE OTHERS MOVE IN ON
HIM. He throws one across the flight deck and
out of the plane. He smashes another with his
shield.
A HUGE PILOT FACES OFF AGAINST STEVE. HE SWINGS
A CHOCK, CLOCKING STEVE IN THE HEAD. STEVE
STAGGERS ONTO A FIGHTER. THE BIG PILOT LEAPS ON
HIM.
Inside the FIGHTER'S COCKPIT, ANOTHER PILOT
sees his chance. He pulls THE RELEASE LEVER...
THE FIGHTER DROPS, WITH STEVE AND THE BIG PILOT
STILL ABOARD.

208 INT./EXT. POD FIGHTER - DAY

Steve holds on as the fighter shoots though the
air. The big pilot hangs on to Steve's boot.
STEVE KICKS. ONCE. TWICE. THE BIG PILOT LOSES
HIS GRIP, TUMBLING INTO THE PROPELLER.
Inside, the fighter pilot looks up, astounded to
see Steve still hanging on.
HE EXECUTES A BARREL-ROLL. STEVE'S EYES ROLL
BACK, SKIN RIPPLING FROM THE G-FORCE.
THE PILOT JERKS THE STICK...BUT STEVE HAULS
HIMSELF FORWARD. HE GRASPS THE EDGE OF THE
COCKPIT AND SLIDES IT OPEN.

The pilot evades Steve's grasping hand. Then
Steve reaches down and PULLS THE EJECTOR SWITCH.
THE PILOT BLASTS INTO THE SKY, SMASHING INTO THE
UNDERSIDE OF THE BOMBER'S WING.
Steve climbs in and hauls on the stick, righting
the plane.

209 INT. SUBORBITAL BOMBER, COCKPIT - DAY

Skull checks AN ELECTRONIC MAP, showing the
plane's progress toward America.
Then he looks out the windshield...AND FREEZES.
STEVE'S RAGGED FIGHTER COMES SWOOPING UP OUT OF
THE CLOUDS, PROPELLER WHIRLING.

210 INT. POD FIGHTER - DAY

Steve yanks the stick, flying shakily toward THE
FLIGHT DECK.

211 INT. SUBORBITAL BOMBER, FLIGHT DECK - DAY

STEVE'S POD-FIGHTER SKIDS ACROSS THE FLIGHT
DECK...FINALLY COMING TO A STOP IN A SHOWER OF
SPARKS AND SCREECHING METAL.
Steve pushes the canopy off and climbs from the
wreck.
He straps on his shield and looks toward THE
COCKPIT...

212 INT. SUBORBITAL BOMBER, COCKPIT - DAY

Steve kicks open the door to find...STILLNESS.
He steps warily toward THE CONTROL PLATFORM. HE
SEES THE PILOT'S CHAIR EMPTY. Suddenly, he hears
THE WHINE OF A HYDRA ASSAULT RIFLE POWERING UP.
His eyes dart to the window, where he sees a
reflection of SKULL AIMING AT HIS BACK.
Steve whips around, shield raised, deflecting
Skull's shot. THE BLAST RICOCHETS, BLOWING OUT A
PANE OF THE COCKPIT GLASS. WIND ROARS.

> RED SKULL
> You don't give up, do you?

> STEVE
> Nope.

Steve charges at Skull, who fires again. Blue
bolts ricochet around the cabin.
Steve swings, bashing the rifle from Skull's
hands. Skull swings. Steve puts Skull in a
headlock. Skull throws Steve into a bulkhead.
STEVE SWINGS HIS SHIELD, BUT SKULL GRABS IT WITH
BOTH HANDS. THE TWO SUPER SOLDIERS STRAIN, EYE
TO EYE.

> RED SKULL
> You wear a flag on your chest and think you
> fight a battle of nations? I have seen the
> future, Captain. There are no flags but
> Hydra's.

> STEVE
> Keep the future. I'm looking for a little
> here and now.

STEVE SLAMS SKULL IN THE JAW WITH THE SHIELD.
SKULL STAGGERS. STEVE COCKS BACK AND HITS SKULL
WITH AN UPPERCUT.
The impact drives Skull up and into...THE
AUTOPILOT CONTROLS.
THE AUTOPILOT DISENGAGES. THE PLANE LURCHES
VIOLENTLY.

212A EXT. SUBORBITAL BOMBER - DAY

THE MASSIVE PLANE SPINS INTO A BARREL ROLL.
Through the cockpit window, we see Steve and
Skull tumbling to the ceiling.

212B INT. SUBORBITAL BOMBER, COCKPIT - DAY

STEVE AND SKULL CRASH ACROSS THE WHIRLING
COCKPIT.
Steve grasps for a handhold.
The plane jerks again, throwing them together.
THEY BATTLE IN CHAOTIC ZERO-G.
Steve powers Skull into the ceiling.
Skull elbows Steve into the wall.
Skull tries to reach the autopilot.
BUT STEVE USES HIS MOMENTUM TO SWING AROUND A
STRUT AND SLAMS HIS SHIELD INTO SKULL'S HEAD.
Skull bashes against the wall, but adeptly
bounces back.
He grabs a strut and kicks Steve toward the back
bulkhead.
Skull flies at the autopilot controls.
WHAM. STEVE SLAMS HARD INTO THE STEEL WALL.
SKULL FINDS A HANDHOLD AND HITS THE AUTOPILOT
BUTTON.

212C EXT. SUBORBITAL BOMBER - DAY

The giant plane pulls out of its dive.

212D INT. SUBORBITAL BOMBER, COCKPIT - DAY

GRAVITY RETURNS with sudden violence.
STEVE SMASHES TO THE FLOOR, HIS SHIELD ROLLING
AWAY.
Steve lies momentarily dazed. His eyes flutter.
Then...

                    RED SKULL (O.S.)
          You could have the power of the gods...

Steve looks up to see Skull advancing, LUGER
DRAWN.

                    RED SKULL (CONT'D)
          And you will not admit you want it?

Standing in front of the cube housing, Skull
takes dead aim at the star on Steve's chest.

>　　　　　　　　STEVE
>　I want what every soldier on every
>　battlefield wants...

Steve eyes the shield at his feet.

>　　　　　　　STEVE (CONT'D)
>　I want to go home.
>　ALT. I want this war to end.

Steve slams his heel onto the shield, flipping it
into the air.
SKULL FIRES.
Steve jumps to his feet, grabbing the shield,
blocking the blast.
He whirls and hurls the shield.
The spinning disc hits Skull in the ribs with a
sickening crunch, knocking him off his feet...
SMASHING HIM INTO THE CUBE CONSOLE.
Blue energy arcs and crackles from the damaged
machinery.
THE ENERGY GAUGE PINS AT OVERLOAD.
Skull pulls himself to his feet, staring in
alarm as...
The cube rises from the machine, glowing with a
violent intensity.
SKULL STARES. HE REACHES OUT AND EXTRACTS THE
CUBE.
STEVE GAPES AS...
THE CUBE BURNS THE GLOVE OFF SKULL'S HAND,
EXPOSING THE SCARRED FLESH.
THE SKULL JUST STARES, OVERCOME AND AMAZED.
Blinded by the light, Steve staggers toward the
controls.
SKULL'S P.O.V.:
THE PLANE SEEMS TO VANISH AROUND HIM.
VISIONS OF THE NINE REALMS DANCE IN THE LIGHT:

A RAINBOW PORTAL STRETCHES PAST AN OBSERVATORY
AND INTO SPACE.

                    RED SKULL
        Valhalla...
        ALT. I was right...
        ALT. It is real...
        ALT. Yes, I understand...
        ALT. I have waited so long...

THE VISIONS SPEED UP UNTIL THEY BLUR. SUDDENLY,
THE CUBE VIBRATES VIOLENTLY.
The Skull looks worried. Something's wrong.

                    RED SKULL (CONT'D)
        No.

STEVE WHIPS UP HIS SHIELD AS ENERGY SHOOTS FROM
THE CUBE.
                    RED SKULL (CONT'D)
        NO!

ENERGY BOLTS RICOCHET OFF THE CEILING AND STRIKE
THE SKULL, VAPORIZING HIM AS...
THE CUBE GOES NOVA.

213 EXT. SUBORBITAL BOMBER - DAY

A MASSIVE COLUMN OF ENERGY SHOOTS TOWARD SPACE,
GROWING IN INTENSITY UNTIL IT EXPLODES OUTWARDS,
EVAPORATING THE CLOUDS. Light glares through the
cockpit windows. Then fades.
The plane whips past.

214 INT. SUBORBITAL BOMBER, COCKPIT - DAY

Steve stands, woozy. When his vision returns,
he sees...THE INERT CUBE. He takes a step toward
it...SUDDENLY, THE PLANE BANKS VIOLENTLY, ITS
ENGINES ROARING.
Steve races for the controls. The forgotten cube

tumbles across the flight deck.
Tink...Tink...Tink...AND FLIES OUT A HOLE IN THE
FUSELAGE.
Steve climbs into the chair.
THE CONTROL STICK steers automatically. Steve
wrestles it, trying to override the plane...BUT
IT WILL NOT ALTER COURSE.
Steve stares at the monitor AND THE GREEN MAP OF
MANHATTAN.

215 INT. HYDRA HQ, CONTROL TOWER - DAY

THE RADIO SQUAWKS in the empty control room.

>   STEVE (ON RADIO)
>   Agent Carter, come in...

Peggy runs in and grabs the radio, frantic and
relieved.

>   PEGGY CARTER
>   Steve, is that you? Are you okay?

>   STEVE (ON RADIO)
>   I'm fine.

THROUGH THE WINDOW, WE SEE THE INVADERS ROUNDING
UP THE SURRENDERED HYDRA MEN.

>   PEGGY CARTER
>   Where's Schmidt?

>   STEVE (ON RADIO)
>   Schmidt's dead.

>   PEGGY CARTER
>   What about the plane?

>   STEVE (ON RADIO)
>   That's a little harder to explain.

INTERCUT:

216 INT. SUBORBITAL BOMBER, COCKPIT - DAY

Steve stares at the New York map, radio in hand. HIS COMPASS lies open on the control board.

> PEGGY CARTER
> Give me your coordinates. I'll find a landing site—

> STEVE
> There isn't going to be a landing. Schmidt's locked the navigation system.

Steve eyes THE REDLINED ENGINE GAUGES in front of him.

> STEVE (CONT'D)
> And there's more than enough power to reach the East Coast.

Peggy looks grave. She waves Colonel Phillips down.

> PEGGY CARTER
> I'll get Howard on the line. He'll know what to do.

> STEVE
> I'm sitting on a hundred tons of explosives. Hotwiring this thing's not an option.

He looks out the window at the vast, blue expanse of ocean.

> STEVE (CONT'D)
> I've got to put her in the water.

Peggy spreads her fingers on the wall, her knuckles white.

> PEGGY CARTER
> But you said you couldn't steer it.

Steve scans the control panel. HE SPOTS A THICK CABLE RUNNING FROM THE IGNITION TO THE ENGINES.

> STEVE
> I can't. But I think I can crash it.

HE YANKS THE CABLE OUT. BLUE SPARKS FLARE. THEN ALL THE LIGHTS DIE. THE ENGINES STOP. THE PLANE GOES QUIET.

> PEGGY CARTER
> Steve, don't do this. We've got time. We can figure this out.

Steve eyes THE NAVIGATION CHARTS.

> STEVE
> I already did. Right now, I'm in the middle of nowhere. If I wait any longer, a lot of people are going to get hurt.
> (beat)
> Peggy, this is my choice.

Peggy and Phillips look at each other, slowly accepting what's happening.

> PEGGY CARTER
> We'll send out rescue ships. We'll find you.

> STEVE
> I don't think there's going to be much left to find.

STEVE LEANS ON THE STICK WITH ALL HIS MIGHT. THE

PLANE BEGINS A SCREAMING DIVE.

                    STEVE (CONT'D)
     Peggy?

                    PEGGY CARTER
     I'm here.

STEVE'S COMPASS SPINS WILDLY. HE JUST STARES AT
HER PICTURE.

                    STEVE
     I'm going to need a raincheck on that
     dance.

                    PEGGY CARTER
     (holding back tears)
     All right. A week Saturday. The Stork
     Club.

                    STEVE
     Okay. You got it.

                    PEGGY CARTER
     8:00 on the dot. If you're three minutes
     late I'm leaving, do you understand?

                    STEVE
     I still don't know how to dance.

She closes her eyes.

                    PEGGY CARTER
     I'll show you. I'll show you everything.
     Just be there.

Clouds whip past the windows as the plane
plummets. STEVE POCKETS THE COMPASS AND SLIDES
HIS MASK OVER HIS FACE. ARCTIC ICE RUSHES UP AT
THE COCKPIT WINDOW.

                         STEVE
         Maybe the band could play something slow.
         I'd hate to step on your—

HISS. The radio in Peggy's hand goes silent.
Colonel Phillips puts a hand on her shoulder.
She just stares out the hangar at the blue sky
beyond.

217 EXT. ARCTIC OCEAN - DAY

THE PLANE SKIDS VIOLENTLY ACROSS A GLACIER. IT
CAREENS OFF THE EDGE AND CRASHES INTO AN ICY
LAKE. The plane floats a moment, then starts to
sink. BLEED IN THE SOUND OF A CHEERING CROWD...

218 EXT. TRAFALGAR SQUARE - DAY

People lean from balconies, holding the V for
Victory sign.
A paper on a newsstand reads, "WAR OVER!"

218A INT. THE WHIP & FIDDLE PUB - DAY

Amidst the revelry, MORITA, JONES, DERNIER,
FALSWORTH and DUGAN stand at attention. Their
bags rest against the wall. THEY SOLEMNLY RAISE
THEIR GLASSES.

219 OMITTED

220 EXT. UNDERWATER - DAY

THE PLANE SINKS SLOWLY IN THE ICY WATER.

220A EXT. STARK SEARCH BOAT - DAY

A TRAWLER bobs on the ocean's surface, at
anchor. All sorts of antennae sprout from the
wheelhouse.

221 INT. STARK SEARCH BOAT, WHEELHOUSE - DAY

HOWARD STARK hunches over a MONITOR on a high-
tech bridge. His assistants eye SONAR and
RADIATION DETECTORS. ONE FEATURES A STEADY GREEN
BLIP.
ON HOWARD'S SCREEN: grainy video footage of the
sea bottom. Sand and fish roll past as the camera
explores the terrain. Howard peers. He stops the
camera sub, adjusts the monitor, bringing into
focus...
THE CRACKED, INERT...COSMIC CUBE.
He operates a pair of joysticks.
ON SCREEN, two robotic claws extend. They reach
out and clasp the cube.
Howard exhales and looks to his assistants.

> HOWARD STARK
> Move us to the next grid point.

> STARK ASSISTANT
> But there's no trace of wreckage, sir. And
> the energy signature stops here.

Stark pushes back from the monitor, spent, grim.

> HOWARD STARK
> Just keep looking.

222 EXT. ARCTIC OCEAN - DAY

THE PLANE'S WINGTIP SLIPS BELOW THE ICE.

223 OMITTED

224 EXT. UNDERWATER - DAY

WE SEE STEVE'S SHADOW THROUGH THE COCKPIT
WINDOW. HE SLUMPS, STRAPPED IN HIS CHAIR.

225 INT. ALLIED HQ - BRIEFING ROOM - DAY

Phillips signs an official report, "CLASSIFIED—
CAPTAIN AMERICA." He stamps it: "INACTIVE."
He slides it into a red box marked "TO BE
DESTROYED." He looks up as Peggy walks in. He
regards her, stoic, suppressing his emotion.

> COLONEL PHILLIPS
> ALT. No one said we have to forget the
> man, Agent.

Peggy nods. She picks up the box and puts it
with others on a table near the door.
For a moment, she just stands there,
overwhelmed. She opens the box, taking out A
PHOTO OF PRE-REBIRTH STEVE. She smiles. Then she
tucks it in her breast pocket. She closes the
box and leaves.

226 EXT. UNDERWATER - DAY

BACK AWAY FROM THE WINDOW UNTIL THE PLANE IS
JUST A SHADOW.

227 EXT. LOWER EAST SIDE - DAY

On a New York street, TWO BOYS PLAY. One fires a
toy gun. The other blocks imaginary bullets with
A GARBAGE CAN LID.

FADE TO BLACK.

After a moment, we can hear, ever so faintly...
THE SOUND OF A BROOKLYN DODGERS GAME ON THE
RADIO.

EXT. 1945 ROOM - DAY

CLOSE ON: STEVE'S FACE. He looks paler,
thinner...but alive.
His eyes flicker open. He sees an old glass

light fixture on a white ceiling. He sits up and finds he's on a bed in a quiet, 1940s room. The sun shines through white curtains. The Dodgers game plays on AN OLD VACUUM TUBE RADIO on a wooden dresser.

> RADIO ANNOUNCER
> "Workman up for the Phillies, now. Holding that big club down at the end. He sets, Chipman pitches. Curveball, outside. Ball one."

Steve slides his bare feet to the worn, wooden floor.

> SSR AGENT
> Good morning.

Steve turns to see A PRETTY 1940S BRUNETTE sitting in a chair. She folds a copy of The Brooklyn Eagle and checks her watch.

> SSR AGENT (CONT'D)
> (smiling gently)
> Or I should say, afternoon.

> STEVE
> I don't...remember going to sleep.

> SSR AGENT
> Well, it was quite a while ago.

Steve rubs his face. The radio plays.

> RADIO ANNOUNCER
> "So the Dodgers are ahead eight to five. And Chipman knows one swing of the bat and this fella's capable of making it a brand new game."

Steve eyes the radio. He takes a long look at her.

                    STEVE
          How long have I been out?

                    RADIO ANNOUNCER
          "Outfield deep, round toward left, the
          infield overshifted."

                    SSR AGENT
          I'm afraid I couldn't say—

With lightning speed, Steve GRABS her arm.

                    SSR AGENT(CONT'D)
          Captain Rogers, please!

                    STEVE
          Who are you? How do you know my name?

                    SSR AGENT
          (wincing)
          We know all about you.

Just then, A LARGE, MENACING MAN in strangely
modern garb rushes into the room. He carries a
set of METAL RESTRAINTS.

                    RADIO ANNOUNCER
          "Here's the pitch from Chipman..."

Steve lets go of the SSR AGENT.
He stares, red-eyed as THE MAN MOVES IN ON
HIM...

                    RADIO ANNOUNCER (CONT'D)
          "Swung on, belted, it's a long one, deep
          into left center, back goes Galan. Back,
          back, back..."

229 INT. HALLWAY - DAY

SUDDENLY, BAM! A DOOR EXPLODES INTO THE HALLWAY,
BLOWN OFF ITS HINGES BY THE FLYING BODY OF THE
MANACLE MAN.
STEVE STAGGERS OUT.

230 OMITTED

231 INT. LOBBY - DAY

Steve races into a busy, modern lobby. SHIELD
operatives stare. MP'S appear ahead of him.

>   SHIELD MP
>   Halt!

Steve bowls them over and runs for the door...

232A EXT. SHIELD HOSPITAL - DAY

Steve bursts outside. He takes a few steps...
THEN STOPS.
MODERN CARS HONK AND ROAR IN THE STREET.
TOWERING PLASMA BILLBOARDS PLAY MOVING ADS
FEATURING LOTS OF FLESH. MODERN PEOPLE RUSH
PAST, IPODS AND CELL PHONES TO THEIR EARS. STEVE
STAGGERS, CONFUSED. HE GLANCES OVER HIS SHOULDER
TO SEE THE MP'S RUSHING OUT. STEVE TAKES OFF,
SPRINTING DOWN THE CROWDED SIDEWALK.

233 EXT. NEW YORK CITY, ALLEYWAY - DAY

Steve skids into an alley and stops, panting,
freaked.
Steve looks down the alley...ONLY TO FIND IT'S A
DEAD END.

>   NICK FURY (O.S.)
>   At ease, soldier.

Steve whips to see...
NICK FURY standing alone at the alley entrance.

> STEVE
>
> Who are you?

> NICK FURY
>
> Colonel Fury, Director of SHIELD. You would
> have known us as the Special Scientific
> Reserve.

Steve's eyes narrow. The first reassuring thing
he's heard.

> STEVE
>
> Where am I?

> NICK FURY
>
> Round about 34th and 5th.

Steve looks confused. Fury nods over his
shoulder at...
THE EMPIRE STATE BUILDING RISING ABOVE THEM.
STEVE GAPES. Fury waves a couple of MP's to
block off the alley. They stand at attention.

> NICK FURY (CONT'D)
>
> Sorry about that little show back there.
> See, there's no precedent for what you've
> been through. We couldn't tell how delicate
> your mental state might be. We thought it
> best to break it to you slowly.

> STEVE
>
> Break what?

> NICK FURY
>
> You've been asleep, Captain. For almost
> seventy years.

Steve looks around, stunned.

>   STEVE
>   Seventy...
>   (sledge-hammered)
>   The World of the Future.

>   NICK FURY
>   Well, thanks to you, there is one.

Steve eyes Fury.

>   STEVE
>   What about the war? Did we win?

>   NICK FURY
>   Hell, yes. Unconditional surrender, baby.
>   And taking down HYDRA was a big part of
>   that.

Steve reels.

>   STEVE
>   How am I...not dead?

>   NICK FURY
>   To be perfectly honest, we're not sure yet.
>   My docs say it's some kind of suspended
>   animation. Dr. Erskine's formula, the
>   extreme cold...I can't break it down for
>   you on a cellular level, but you haven't
>   aged a day since that plane went down.

Steve looks around, overwhelmed. Above him, a
highway sign reads "FDR DRIVE, NEXT LEFT."

>   NICK FURY (CONT'D)
>   You don't mind my asking, what gave us
>   away back there?

                    STEVE
What? Oh. Bob Chipman was traded for Eddie
Stanky during the '44 season. He's with
the Cubs now.
(troubled)
Or...was.

                    NICK FURY
I know it's a lot to swallow. But the
world's not as different as it looks.
There's still work to be done...
(pointed)
Soldier's work.

Steve meets Fury's eyes. Fury signals to one of
the MP's.
He brings forward A CASE. Fury opens it,
revealing STEVE'S BATTERED SHIELD.

                    NICK FURY (CONT'D)
The world could still use a man like you,
Cap.

Steve touches the shield, remembering.

                    NICK FURY (CONT'D)
Take your time. God knows if anybody's
earned it, you have. All the same...

Fury offers his hand. Steve takes it.

                    NICK FURY (CONT'D)
There's a place for you on the team.

Steve rubs his head, so many things coming back.

                    NICK FURY (CONT'D)
You sure you're all right?

                    STEVE
Yeah. It's just...

PUSH IN on Steve's stunned face.

                 STEVE (CONT'D)
     (quietly)
     I had a date.

FADE OUT.

KRUGER CHASE SCENE

storyboards by Rodolfo Damaggio

When Operation: Rebirth — the program responsible for transforming Steve Rogers from a frail weakling into an idealized human specimen — erupts into violence due to the actions of German spy Heinz Kruger, Rogers and Peggy Carter are quick to respond. Rogers' new body is put to the test as he takes off on foot after Kruger's taxi.

SHOT 37

SHOT 41

STEVE LOSES CONTROL OF
HIS NEW RUNNING ABILITIES

ALLEY OUT

TAXI OUT

POLLY W/ PAN
FROM OUT OF ALLEYWAY
TOWARDS WINDOW

(19)

DOLLY W/STEVE
AS HE PASSES BY
CAM. OUT OF CONTROL

ONE SHOT

SHOT 56

Old Driver

KRUGER CUTS
OFF INTERSECTION

DRIVER SWERVES
INTO STREET

SHOT 57

SHOT 58

Ⓐ

Ⓑ

 STEVE OUT

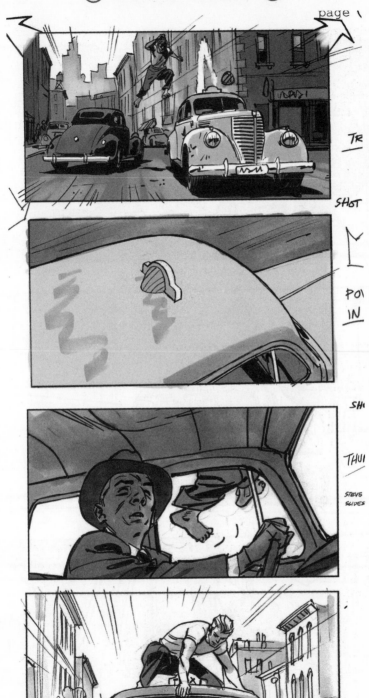

page \

TR

SHOT

POI
IN

SH

THU

STEVE
SLIDES

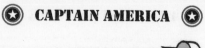